Learn Like a Lobster

Learn Like a Lobster

Grow as You Go,
Fuel Your Own Progress,
Accelerate Your Career

Helen Tupper
and Sarah Ellis

PENGUIN LIFE

AN IMPRINT OF

PENGUIN BOOKS

PENGUIN LIFE

UK | USA | Canada | Ireland | Australia
India | New Zealand | South Africa

Penguin Life is part of the Penguin Random House group of companies whose addresses can be found at global.penguinrandomhouse.com

Penguin Random House UK,
One Embassy Gardens, 8 Viaduct Gardens, London SW11 7BW

penguin.co.uk

First published 2026
003

Copyright © Helen Tupper and Sarah Ellis, 2026

The moral right of the copyright holders has been asserted

Thank you to Laura K. Corless for the book design

Penguin Random House values and supports copyright.
Copyright fuels creativity, encourages diverse voices, promotes freedom of expression and supports a vibrant culture. Thank you for purchasing an authorized edition of this book and for respecting intellectual property laws by not reproducing, scanning or distributing any part of it by any means without permission. You are supporting authors and enabling Penguin Random House to continue to publish books for everyone.
No part of this book may be used or reproduced in any manner for the purpose of training artificial intelligence technologies or systems. In accordance with Article 4(3) of the DSM Directive 2019/790, Penguin Random House expressly reserves this work from the text and data mining exception

Set in 11.88/17.17 pt Sabon MT Pro
Typeset by Six Red Marbles UK, Thetford, Norfolk
Printed and bound in Great Britain by Clays Ltd, Elcograf S.p.A.

The authorized representative in the EEA is Penguin Random House Ireland, Morrison Chambers, 32 Nassau Street, Dublin D02 YH68

A CIP catalogue record for this book is available from the British Library

HARDBACK ISBN: 978–0–241–71895–7
TRADE PAPERBACK ISBN: 978–0–241–71900–8

Penguin Random House is committed to a sustainable future for our business, our readers and our planet. This book is made from Forest Stewardship Council® certified paper

To Nanny – the lobster that never stops learning and who always supports me to grow

To Rob – for being our first reader and reviewer, you kept me going and growing

CONTENTS

Introduction: A surprising role model for learning — 1

PART 1: Learn as you go — 9
    Chapter 1: Learning from everyday experiments — 13
    Chapter 2: Questions that uncover learning — 33
    Chapter 3: Data for your development — 55

PART 2: Learn in hard moments — 87
    Chapter 4: Feedback that puts learning first — 91
    Chapter 5: How to learn when things go wrong — 127

PART 3: Lead your own learning — 169
    Chapter 6: Seven ways to lead your own learning — 175

PART 4: Lobster-like learners — 233
    Chapter 7: Advice from lobster-like learners — 235

Grow your own way — 245
Acknowledgements — 247
Endnotes — 249
Index — 253

INTRODUCTION

A Surprising Role Model for Learning

'People seldom improve when they have no other model but themselves to copy.'

Oliver Goldsmith

At the start of writing this book we knew a lot about learning and a little about lobsters. A friend had mentioned that lobsters never stopped growing, and this insight intrigued us. When we dived a bit deeper into the life of a lobster, we discovered that they have three distinctive characteristics that make them a surprising role model for learning:

- Lobsters never stop growing.
- Lobsters grow in hard moments.
- Lobsters fuel their own growth.

We started to spot the parallels between the life of a lobster and the life of a learner.

- Learners are always a work in progress and never stop developing.
- Learners see challenges as a chance to grow in new ways.
- Learners don't wait, but create their own opportunities to grow.

It turns out that learning like a lobster is a good way to guarantee our growth at work. Just like the lobster never stops growing, the best learners are always improving and never settle for where they are today.

The importance of learning at work isn't new. We've always needed to develop if we want to do well in our jobs. What's different now is how quickly our work is changing; as a result, our skills need constant updating to make sure we stay relevant. Learning is essential in our roles – both now, and to create possibilities for our future.

> **The problem isn't convincing ourselves that learning is important but working out how to make it happen.**

The reality of a working week means that learning often doesn't make it onto our to-do list. Even when it does, there's always a more pressing priority that takes our time and attention. The practicalities of learning at work continue to get in the way of our growth, but we can't rely on what we know today to get us where we want to go in the future.

Letting Go of Ladder-Like Learning

Careers used to be linear and ladder-like. They were about following in other people's footsteps, and focused on getting to the top. Learning was limited by level, and there was little need to be curious about your own career beyond taking the next step. This hundred-year-old approach to careers is no longer fit for purpose; it doesn't reflect people's reality or their individuality. Today our careers are characterized by change and choices, by potential and possibilities. Climbing the ladder step-by-step has been replaced by something more 'squiggly'.

'Human beings are works in progress that mistakenly think they're finished.'
Dan Gilbert

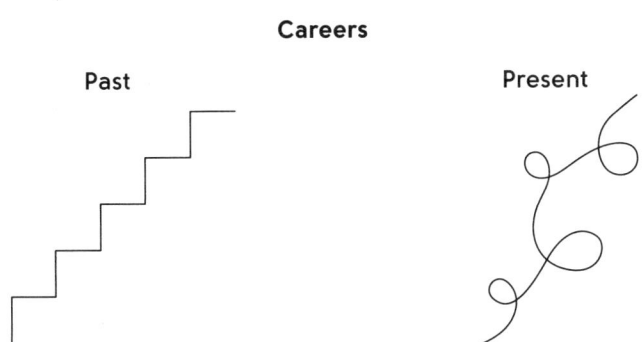

Careers

Past   Present

The Squiggly Career

In a squiggly career you're always learning and growing. You create possibilities and you're curious about the different directions in which you can develop. You recognize that there's no such thing as a straight line to success, and you have the skills to overcome obstacles and make the most of opportunities. Instead of subscribing to one view of what a 'good' career looks like, a squiggly career is as unique as you are.

We created the concept of squiggly careers in 2013 and found that it quickly connected with people who felt it reflected their experiences and ambitions. Since then, we've written two bestselling books, run hundreds of training programmes across the world and produced over 500 weekly podcasts. Through supporting more than 5 million people to succeed in their squiggly career, one skill has consistently stood out as the biggest contributor to people's success: their ability to learn.

> **Successful learners are defined by how, not what, they learn.**

The best learners are curious, open and intentional about their learning. Where others stall and get stuck, these learners find a way to keep growing. And their investment in learning pays off. They have more opportunities, find their way through challenges, and create possibilities for their future. By always learning, they're always growing.

Everyone can learn like a lobster, but many people feel constrained by the ladder-like learning that is still common in lots of workplaces. These are environments where learning is linear, linked to your job title and often limited to going on a course. Lobster-like learners have spotted that this way of learning needs to be left behind. They focus on developing their talents and learning in a way that's personal to them and their progression.

These learners use experiments to test their knowledge, rather than feeling pressured to prove their expertise. They ask questions, rather than assume they know the right answer. Success in a squiggly career now relies on learning like a lobster and stepping off the outdated learning ladder. This success shows up in more than one way. Learners are proven to be more likely to lead, benefit from a wider range of opportunities for progression, and earn more over the course of their career.[1]

Lobster-like learners stay relevant and resilient because they never stop growing.

Ladder-like learning	Lobster-like learning
Titles	Talents
Permission	Personalized
Waiting	Creating
Occasional	Everyday
Expert	Experiment
Assume	Ask

How to Learn Like a Lobster

We have one goal for this book: that by learning like a lobster you'll grow in your career. We've divided the book into four parts.

- Part 1: Learn as you go
- Part 2: Learn in hard moments
- Part 3: Lead your own learning
- Part 4: Lobster-like learners

In Part 1, we focus on how you can learn more from your role in a way that's realistic and easy to do. We cover *everyday experiments*, *questions* and *data for your development*. When you learn as you go, you increase your impact and stay relevant in your role.

In Part 2, we focus on how to learn in hard moments. We cover *feedback that puts learning first* and *learning when things go wrong*. Being able to learn in a hard moment means you can respond with resilience. Challenges and tough times are inevitable, but looking for the learning in these hard moments will help you to grow faster and go further.

In Part 3, we explore how to lead your own learning, rather than waiting for it to come your way. We share *seven different ways to create your learning* – from being a beginner to finding moments for play. Leading your own learning means you will create more opportunities to grow in your career.

In Part 4, we share advice from a variety of lobster-like learners – from fashion designers to Olympians and CEOs. We asked everyone to answer the same question: *What advice would you give to someone who wants to learn more at work?* By bringing together their insights at the end of the book we hope to leave you with even more inspiration for your learning.

Learn Like a Lobster will motivate you to work in a different way, helping you to have a career that is as individual as you are. A career where you find your work fulfilling and feel proud of the impact you have. Learning like a lobster is how you make that happen. It's how you stay relevant, resilient and create new opportunities.

Because when you learn, you grow.

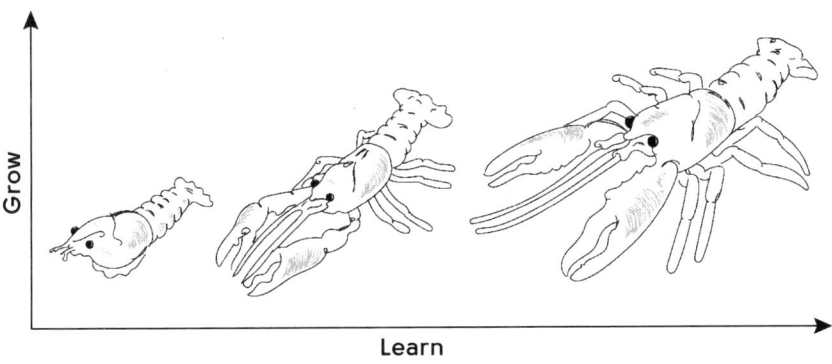

Part 1

Learn as You Go

'Learning is a constant process of discovery – a process without end.'

Bruce Lee

You don't have to look too hard to start discovering why the lobster is a useful, if surprising, role model for learning. A lobster never stops growing, and this endless growth continues throughout its long life.

Though continuous growth isn't unique to lobsters, what makes them special is how their growth happens. For most creatures the size of their shell limits their chance to grow, but lobsters have found a clever way around this constraint. By repeatedly shedding its shell, in a process known as 'moulting', the lobster benefits from never-ending growth. During each moult the length of a lobster increases by up to 15 per cent and its weight can double. Young lobsters can moult up to five times a year, and though the lobster sheds its shell less frequently as it ages, it never stops. This lifelong growth is a key part of how lobsters not only survive but flourish.

One of the lobster's claims to fame is that it holds the record for the world's heaviest marine crustacean, weighing in at 20kgs and more than a metre in length.[2]

> **A lobster never settles in the shell that it has; it grows as it goes.**

We have more in common with the lobster than we might imagine. Though our bodies stop growing, our brains don't. Where lobsters have moulting to thank for their growth, we have a process called 'neuroplasticity', which is the brain's ability to adapt and change in response to our experiences. Our brains are not fixed; we have an inbuilt capacity to keep learning and growing. We learn all the time through the experiences and situations that make up our days and weeks at work. However, unlike the lobster, we can choose to deliberately learn and take advantage of our brain's endless capacity for growth.

> **Default learning happens every day, but deciding how much you want to learn and grow is ultimately up to you.**

Why Learning as You Go Will Help You Grow

There are learning moments every day at work, but when we miss the moment, we miss out on learning. Learning as you go looks like taking easy and small actions that add up to lots of learning over time. It means adding learning *into* your day not adding learning *onto* your day. This could look like asking different kinds of questions in the meetings you're already in, or experimenting with new ways to think through some of the challenges in your role.

When you learn as you go, you never get left behind.

Learning as you go doesn't rely on being less busy, or require a dramatic change in how you spend your time at work. Learning is not separate to the job that you do; learning is part of doing your job.

What Gets in the Way of Learning as You Go

How we label learning makes a difference to our development. It can be hard to let go of our default idea that learning looks like going on a course or gaining a new qualification. We might be used to our learning being defined by the title we have or the level of seniority we've reached. And it's true that learning is easier to identify when it's separate from our day jobs and visible in our diaries. But this narrow perspective of what learning looks like will limit your growth, and you'll miss out on lots of learning along the way.

When learning becomes part of how we do our job, it is an inevitable outcome of everything we do. Each meeting, moment, conversation and presentation becomes an opportunity to grow. When we learn like a lobster, we never stop learning and never stop growing.

How to Learn as You Go

No one needs a bigger list of actions, but you don't need to work harder or longer to learn more at work. We can find ways to learn as we go – every day, week, month and year. In Part 1 we focus on three areas to support you to learn more from the work you already do.

1. Experiments: testing and learning from everyday actions
2. Questions: asking questions to uncover learning
3. Data: collecting data for your development

> 'Learn continually – there's always "one more thing" to learn!' STEVE JOBS

EXPERT INSIGHT: HEAVY LEARNERS

Research into 'heavy learners' by Josh Bersin found that the more you learn, the better you feel and the more value you add. Heavy learners – defined as people who spend time learning in their day-to-day roles – were measurably more engaged, productive and successful. Specifically, a heavy learner was 74 per cent more likely to know where they want to go in their career, 48 per cent more likely to have found purpose in their work and 47 per cent less likely to be stressed.[3]

CHAPTER 1

Learning from Everyday Experiments

'Experimentation is the least arrogant method of gaining knowledge.'

Isaac Asimov

Every experiment starts without knowing quite where you'll end up. You might have an idea of what you hope to prove but, by definition, experiments are designed for learning, exploring unknowns and figuring out what works and what doesn't.

Experiments move us forward and advance our understanding. Naming and labelling some of our learning as an experiment changes both our frame of mind and our approach. We give ourselves permission to try things out, and we remove the pressure to be perfect. We discover a playfulness and freedom that facilitate learning.

For example, saying to ourselves *I'm experimenting with new ways to approach meetings* feels very different to *I need to completely rethink how I run meetings*. In the first instance we feel intrigued, curious and creative, whereas in the second we're more likely to feel stuck or daunted.

'The words we use frame how we see the world.'
LUDWIG WITTGENSTEIN

Experiments Lead to Learning

Spotting opportunities to experiment as part of the work we already do is a simple yet significant way to design learning into our days. Experiments are an intentional way to interrupt our status quo and mean we can spot opportunities for continual improvement. When we start experimenting, we uncover more possibilities for learning. Rather than relying on our existing assumptions, we test our thinking. We let go of there being one way or a right way to do something and instead focus on exploring and discovery.

Learn-as-You-Go Experiments

Experiments come in all shapes and sizes and our aim is to design ones that are easy to try out as part of the work that you already do. If an experiment is too ambitious, you're less likely to give it a go; if it's too time-consuming, your to-do list will stop you before you get started.

When we experiment, the focus is not on whether we're right first time but on whether we learn something as a result.

An experiment only fails if we fail to learn.

One watch-out when experimenting is not considering how you will capture your learning along the way. Keeping notes on your experiments is a simple part of the process, but one that's easy to overlook. If we experiment but miss writing down what we learn, we've wasted our time and effort. Keeping a note of what you learn means you reflect on what's been useful and have something to refer back to.

There are two essential design features of a learn-as-you-go experiment.

1. **Easy:** can be tried out quickly and easily.
2. **Everyday:** can be added to what you already do.

Spotting Opportunities to Experiment

A useful place to start with designing a learn-as-you-go experiment is to identify a recurring frustration in your week, where the solution for what to do differently isn't obvious. We've selected three familiar frustrations which hold lots of opportunities for experimenting and learning.

1. I don't have time to think in my week.
2. I have too many meetings and they don't feel useful.
3. I'm not making progress on my priorities.

For each of these frustrations we've shared two experiments for you to try. You might want to try one experiment or two together, as one experiment often leads to another. You can also adapt the experiments and create your own. The most important action is that you start experimenting.

LEARNING FROM EVERYDAY EXPERIMENTS

I don't have time to think in my week		
Experiments	To-think lists	Out-loud and quiet thinking
I have too many meetings and they don't feel useful		
Experiments	Decision/discussion agendas	Subtraction
I'm not making progress on my priorities		
Experiments	Minimum useful progress	No-cabulary

Frustration:
'I Don't Have Time to Think in My Week'

Most of us would like more time to think – whether that's thinking through a small improvement or a significant change – but the demands of our work can get in the way. We're left feeling that thinking time is a privilege reserved for certain people or positions, rather than something that's available to everyone.

Giving up on thinking is giving up on learning.

To learn as we go, we need to think as we go. It's unrealistic to imagine we can suddenly add hours of contemplation to our schedules. So instead, we'll explore experiments that can make thinking a possibility even in the busiest of weeks.

Experiment 1: *to-think lists*
Experiment 2: *out-loud and quiet thinking*

The aim of these experiments is to create clarity on *what* to think about, and *how* to think in a way that fits into your week. We all have times where we feel confused, overwhelmed or unsure. Rather than feeling stuck in this state, finding ways to think things through will mean you can quickly move from uncertainty to clarity.

> **'In a world deluged by irrelevant information, clarity is power.'** YUVAL NOAH HARARI

EXPERIMENT 1: TO-THINK LISTS

Lots of people have a to-do list, but how many of us have a to-think list? A to-think list is an easy way to provide a focus for your thoughts and create clarity on what you want to think about. You might have a long list, so themes are a useful way to get started. We'd also suggest writing a to-think list using questions, as this provides a prompt for our brains to start searching for potential answers.

HOW TO EXPERIMENT WITH A TO-THINK LIST

Step 1: write a to-think list in the same place as your to-do list so it's unmissable.

Step 2: circle the question you want to focus on first.

Step 3: look at your week ahead and identify when you have a meeting or moment to focus on exploring a question on your to-think list.

EXAMPLES OF TO-THINK LISTS

To-think list: role

How can I stretch my strengths to increase my impact?

Who influences my objectives and outcomes?

What is causing this challenge on my project?

To-think list: career progression

What career possibilities am I curious to learn more about?

Who could connect me to opportunities I'm interested in?

What do I want to be true in twelve months' time that isn't true today?

To-think list: professional profile

What do I want to build a reputation for?

How could I raise my profile?

What can I learn from people I admire?

EXPERIMENT 2: OUT-LOUD AND QUIET THINKING

> 'Thinking better than others means you'll have more free time and fewer problems.' SHANE PARRISH

Experimenting with a to-think list gives us a focus for *what* to think about, whereas this second experiment is designed to explore *how* to think things through. If we always think in the same way – for example, by running our thoughts past a trusted colleague – it means we miss out on generating alternative answers to a question we want to explore, or gaining clarity in an area of confusion.

There is value in both thinking out loud, where we share our thoughts with other people, and quiet thinking, where we think by ourselves. It's interesting to experiment with a range of different thinking styles rather than relying on one approach. This will increase your options and the likelihood of being able to create time to think quickly. Though you might prefer to think out loud with someone, if they're not available you could try a voice note to yourself. Or you can use a meeting you already have in the diary to share some first thoughts with someone in your team.

Out-loud thinking	Quiet thinking
Voice notes to other people	Voice notes to yourself
Walk and talk with a colleague	A solo walk with no distractions
Saying to someone, 'Can I share some first thoughts with you?'	Saying to yourself, 'What do I think about this?'
Sharing a Miro or Mural board with someone with your initial ideas	Creating a mind map to capture the ideas you've got

EXPERT INSIGHT: THE SKILL OF SELF-EXPLAINING

Author and researcher Ulrich Boser shares an effective and often overlooked learning strategy: self-explaining. This is the ability to ask yourself explanatory questions like, 'What does this mean?' or, 'Why does this matter?' combined with saying the answers out loud to yourself. One study found that people who explain things to themselves learn almost three times more than those who don't.[4] Boser points out that talking to ourselves requires us to slow down, which makes us more deliberate in our reflections, and this means we gain more from our experiences.[5] Momentarily pausing to talk to ourselves helps us to focus on our thinking, make connections and improve our understanding of what's happening.

Frustration:
'I Have Too Many Meetings and They Don't Feel Useful'

Meetings are where we spend lots of our time at work, but they're rarely the moments in our week we most look forward to or expect to learn lots from. In fact, research suggests our relationship with meetings is becoming increasingly negative:

- 70 per cent of people believe that their job satisfaction would increase if they could attend fewer meetings.
- The average time spent in meetings tripled between 2020 and 2022.
- Meetings are rated as the number one killer of productivity.

Learning from Everyday Experiments

In 2023 tech company Shopify, who have 10,000 employees, decided that meetings had become such a drain on people's days that they designed a bot to delete all recurring meetings with three or more people. This meant 322,000 hours of meetings disappeared, the equivalent of adding 150 more people to the organization. Employees were asked to wait for two weeks before adding any critical meetings back in. Perhaps unsurprisingly, most meetings didn't make the cut.

Getting together with people is an important part of how work gets done, and it's unlikely that meetings will entirely disappear from our calendars. However, some small experiments can increase the usefulness of meetings, both for you and the people you work with.

Experiment 1: *decision/discussion agendas*
Experiment 2: *subtraction*

Experimenting with meetings is a chance to refocus on collaboration. Collaboration at its best is the chance to work with people to build something better than you could achieve by yourself. By collaborating we benefit from other people's insights, knowledge and ideas and, in turn, expand how much we learn in the roles that we do.

Every person we work with is someone we can learn from.

EXPERT INSIGHT: COLLABORATION OVERLOAD

In some organizations collaboration is causing overload. Employees are pressured by competing demands and the need to keep up with the proliferation of collaborative technologies. Researchers suggest that in most organizations collaborative work is badly managed, and this creates significant inefficiencies, for example:

- **Double-booked meetings:** in one organization studied, half of all meetings on employees' calendars were double-booked with other meetings.
- **Fractured time:** employees at three Fortune 500 companies toggled between apps more than 1,200 times per day.

Recognizing these challenges, some organizations now explicitly document how to use technology for collaboration, providing a clear framework for what to use, and when. Others have introduced focus time or 'Meeting Doomsday' where a complete reset of collaborative practices takes place.[6]

EXPERIMENT 1: DECISION/DISCUSSION AGENDAS

We all appreciate that meetings need agendas to avoid becoming vague and unwieldy. However, an agenda by itself isn't enough to make meetings more productive. Instead of writing a traditional agenda with a list of bullet points, try experimenting with an alternative agenda that covers the areas for discussion or decisions that need to be made. This focuses everyone's mind on the conversation that needs to happen, and means people can prepare and contribute more meaningfully.

EXAMPLE OF A TYPICAL AGENDA VERSUS DECISION AND DISCUSSION AGENDA

Typical agenda	Decision agenda	Discussion agenda
1. People update 2. Cash flow overview 3. Review project progress 4. AOB	1. Do we hire person A or B? 2. Do we continue to invest in pilot, based on cash flow? 3. Go/no-go decision, based on project progress	1. Explore ideas for attracting a wider range of talent 2. Share ideas for cost savings 3. Discuss risks to project progress

EXPERT INSIGHT: WATCH OUT FOR OVERRATING YOUR OWN MEETINGS

Meeting expert and researcher Steven G. Rogelberg points out that leaders consistently rate their own meetings favourably and much more positively than attendees do. For example, a survey of more than 1,300 managers found that 79 per cent described their own meetings as 'extremely' or 'very' productive, compared to 56 per cent who said the same about meetings initiated by others.[7] Rogelberg points out that hardly any organizations measure meeting effectiveness, despite this accounting for a significant portion of people's time and energy. Rogelberg suggests that 'the goal should be not to kill all meetings but to eliminate the ineffective or unnecessary ones and improve the quality of those that remain'.

🔊 Learn more by listening to episode 392 of the *Squiggly Careers* podcast: *How to Make Every Meeting Matter*.

EXPERIMENT 2: SUBTRACTION

We might not be in the position to follow in Shopify's footsteps by deleting all meetings and starting again from scratch, but we can still experiment with subtracting. This means challenging our assumptions about what a meeting needs to look like. The idea here is to experiment with taking something away from a meeting, to see what impact it has.

> EXAMPLES OF MEETING SUBTRACTIONS
>
> - **Stop going to one meeting:** you could try using AI to create a summary of the meeting so you stay up to date with what's happening.
> - **Make a meeting ten minutes shorter:** this might help you to have a more focused conversation.
> - **Delete a recurring meeting:** looking for meetings that have become more habitual than helpful is a good place to start.
> - **Take the chairs away and have a stand-up meeting:** spot a short meeting, such as a daily huddle or a team meeting, where energy is important.
> - **Reduce the number of people attending:** try experimenting with no more than five people in any meeting.

Frustration:
'I'm Not Making Progress on My Priorities'

The demands on our days can make it hard to move our priorities forward. Working on multiple projects and in cross-functional teams pulls our attention in different directions. It often feels difficult to figure out what matters most, and it's easy to fall into the trap of progressing other people's priorities rather than our own. Our days get derailed by saying yes to whatever comes our way, and we nudge lots of smaller tasks along rather than delivering on the work that makes the most difference.

We can also get in our own way. A desire to make things perfect means we find it hard to spot when good enough is great. This slows us down, as we treat everything as equally important. Whether your frustrations at not making progress are caused by other people or yourself, the aim of these next experiments is to locate the signal amongst the noise and focus on what matters in your role.

Experiment 1: *minimum useful progress*
Experiment 2: *no-cabulary*

EXPERT INSIGHT:
ARE YOU A PERFECTIONIST?

Two Canadian psychologists, Paul Hewitt and Gordon Flett, identified that perfectionism is more than just setting high goals or standards. It's about how you see yourself and interpret what others say and do. Together they developed a self-reporting measure of perfectionism, using three core elements:

1. Self-orientated perfectionism: **the irrational desire to be perfect.**

    I aim to be as perfect as I can be.

2. **Socially prescribed perfectionism:** our environment demands perfection.

   I feel that others are too demanding of me to be perfect.

3. **Other-orientated perfectionism:** imposing unrealistic standards on other people.

   I expect other people to do things perfectly.

As psychologist Thomas Curran shares in his TED talk, socially prescribed perfectionism is on the rise and results in a sense of both helplessness and, even worse, hopelessness. He concludes his talk by saying that we all need to encourage each other to 'celebrate the joys and the beauties of imperfection as a normal and natural part of everyday living and loving'.

🔊 Learn more by listening to episode 73 of the *Squiggly Careers* podcast: *How to Stop Perfectionism Holding You Back*.

EXPERIMENT 1: MINIMUM USEFUL PROGRESS

> 'The main thing is to keep the main thing the main thing.' STEPHEN COVEY

A need for perfection can get in the way of making progress. We hold onto work too tightly, for too long, or perhaps avoid getting started until we're completely 'ready'. Making progress on priorities means recognizing when good enough is great, and learning to let work go.

This experiment starts with an uncomfortable question: *What's the least I can do on this piece of work before usefully sharing it with someone else?*

The purpose of this question is to challenge ourselves to complete only the minimum amount of work possible before sharing it with someone else.

This experiment can be particularly helpful for making progress on something you feel emotionally attached to, or when you tend to keep tweaking so something is 'just right' before sharing. By telling someone about your MUP experiment you'll also consolidate your commitment and resist the urge to revert to your usual approach. This is as simple as saying to your manager, 'I'll share my first draft of a project with you by the end of the week. That way, we'll be able to review it together in our next 121.'

WHEN GOOD ENOUGH IS GREAT

Task	Perfection	Minimum Useful Progress
Update on a project	Full presentation deck with all the information someone needs	Project on a page – a summary of the why, what and how for a project
Gather ideas from team	A two-hour virtual workshop session to discuss and debate ideas	A Miro board – where people can share initial ideas using virtual Post-it notes
Customer experience update for senior team	In-depth walk-through of the customer experience	Stages sketch – draw out and connect key moments of the customer journey
First draft of a report	Detailed report: all available data and recommendations in one document	Headers only – write the headers for a report but no content

EXPERT INSIGHT:
COMEDIANS IN PROGRESS

In the comedy world 'work in progress' shows are common. These shows are intentionally half formed, and it's not unusual to see a comedian arrive onstage with notes and a pen in hand. Through these gigs, comedians have made sharing their minimum viable progress an integral, and very transparent, part of how they do their job. Audiences are an essential part of shaping the finished product, and how a comedian figures out whether something is as funny out loud as they'd imagined in their head. As *Guardian* journalist Brian Logan shares, a work in progress show gives performers flexibility 'to present something unfinished, to experiment with ideas that may not make the finished show, to be less good, frankly, than they'd feel obliged to be in a battle-ready new show'.[8]

EXPERIMENT 2: NO-CABULARY

> 'The real measure of any time management technique is whether or not it helps you neglect the right things.' OLIVER BURKEMAN

When other people make a request for your time, an outright 'no' rarely feels like the right answer. This might be because you're a natural people pleaser, so your default is to help and say 'yes' without pausing for thought. Or you could be worried about the potential for confrontation that comes with saying no. The person asking also influences how hard it feels to say no, especially if they are in a position of power or more senior than you.

Learning from Everyday Experiments

This experiment involves practising saying no in a way that feels right for you. A no-cabulary reflects different ways of saying no, depending on the situation. Sometimes saying no can be a quick, instant message; in other moments it might be saying no during a conversation with your manager.

NO-CABULARY

- **Not me:** explaining why you're not the right fit for the request being made.
- **Not now:** challenging the immediacy of the request to see if it can wait.
- **Not that way:** suggesting alternative ways to achieve the request.

EXAMPLES OF NO-CABULARY

The 'Not Me' No

I don't think I'm the right person to lead that piece of work. I can suggest a couple of other people who might be able to offer support.

The 'Not Now' No

I won't get to that this week as I'm focusing on project A, but I will have space next week. How does that sound?

The 'Not That Way' No

I'm not able to offer a mentoring session at the moment, as I'm focused on writing our next book. I am happy to leave you a voice note with a few thoughts if that would work for you instead?

What Will I Learn?

Experimenting is how we learn to solve problems in new ways.

Problems are part of work. No process is perfect, all projects have unexpected issues, and people are unpredictable. When faced with a problem, we feel pressure to find a solution, but answers are not always obvious. Experimenting takes the pressure of a problem away. Instead of looking for a perfect solution, the focus shifts to finding opportunities to learn. To try out a small, easy action and learn what works, what doesn't, and what to do differently next time.

When we experiment, we move from complaining about a problem to being curious about what we could do differently. The more we experiment, the more we learn, and the less likely problems are to get in the way of our growth.

LEARNING FROM EVERYDAY EXPERIMENTS: SUMMARY

1. Experiments are designed for learning. They give us permission to try things out without the pressure to be perfect. The only experiment that fails is one where we fail to learn.

2. Familiar frustrations – including not enough time to think, too many meetings, and not making progress on our priorities – provide a useful starting point for experimenting.

3. Thinking things through is how we move from uncertainty and confusion to clarity. Experimenting with a to-think list will help you identify what you want to think about, and out-loud/quiet thinking will give you a range of ways to fit thinking into your week.

4. Meetings are moments to collaborate and learn from other people. Decision/discussion agendas and subtracting give you ways to experiment with increasing the usefulness of meetings.

5. People and perfectionism can slow down the progress we make on our priorities. Experimenting with minimum useful progress and your no-cabulary helps you to stay focused on what matters most.

6. Problems are part of work. Experimenting takes the pressure of solving a problem away and prompts us to view frustrations with curiosity and as a chance to learn.

DIVE INTO LEARNING LIKE A LOBSTER
- Begin by: writing a to-think list.
- Then try: a decision and discussion agenda for your next meeting.

CHAPTER 2

Questions That Uncover Learning

'Without questions there is no learning.'
W. Edwards Deming

We ask lots of autopilot questions at work, relying on and repeating the ones that feel comfortable and familiar. But when we are motivated by learning, we start to ask different kinds of questions. Questions where we might be surprised by the answers, and ones which create a deeper level of connection with our colleagues. Questions that are led by curiosity, understanding and openness.

We have the chance to practise asking questions every day, and some simple and small changes to your approach will turn into lots more learning.

In this chapter we cover three ways of asking questions to learn more as you go:

1. **Coach yourself questions:** to increase self-awareness and identify actions that accelerate learning

2. **Situational questions:** to adapt so you don't get stuck
3. **Conversational questions:** to learn more from the conversations you already have with managers, mentors, peers and team members

Coach Yourself Questions

> 'This inner voice that we have is not something we want to rid ourselves of. It's something we want to harness.' ETHAN KROSS

Coach yourself questions give you the opportunity to collect small, specific insights that will increase your self-awareness. Self-awareness is the ability to see ourselves clearly, to understand what motivates and drives us, and to recognize how our behaviour impacts other people. It's a learnable and critical skill for our careers, but it can feel hard to pin down what that skill looks like in an average week at work. We don't have time to dedicate to soul-searching, so self-awareness becomes a skill that feels important to improve, but hard to practically make happen. Asking coach yourself questions is a practical and efficient way to understand yourself and to reflect on your everyday experiences. It means that we can quickly connect self-awareness to actions that accelerate our learning.

Questions That Uncover Learning

> 'I think self-awareness is probably the most important thing towards being a champion.'
> BILLIE JEAN KING

Three Principles of Coach Yourself Questions

PRINCIPLE 1: OPEN

Open questions work because they prompt us to go beyond a binary yes/no response. For example, you learn much more from, 'How would I describe my relationship with my manager?' versus, 'Have I got a good relationship with my manager?'

Using the '5Ws and 1H' is an easy way to guarantee an open question:

5Ws + 1H = who, what, where, when, why and how

(though watch out for *why*, which you can read about in the next expert insight)

EXAMPLES OF 'OPEN' COACH YOURSELF QUESTIONS

Who could help me think through this challenge?
What is one way I could increase my influence?
Where do I make the biggest difference to my team?
When was I at my best today?
Why do I feel this way?
How could I improve the meetings I'm in?

EXPERT INSIGHT:
WATCH OUT FOR 'WHY?' QUESTIONS

In research with nearly 5,000 people, organizational psychologist Tasha Eurich discovered that asking ourselves a 'why' question (for example, 'Why am I not getting along with my manager?') is a surprisingly ineffective way to increase our self-awareness. Eurich shares three challenges if we start a question with 'why':

1. Our answers are wrong: We tend to invent answers that feel true but are often wrong.
2. Our confidence that our wrong answers are right: We don't question how valid or free from bias our reflections are, and we ignore evidence that suggests we might be wrong.
3. 'Why' questions prompt negative thoughts: When we ask ourselves 'why', it's easy to get trapped in a cycle of rumination and become focused on our fears and shortcomings.

Highly self-aware people – which, according to Eurich's research, is only about 15 per cent of us – ask 'what' rather than 'why' questions. For example, asking, 'What can I do to improve my relationship with my manager?' rather than, 'Why is my manager so difficult?' prompts us to focus on actions that are within our control.

Eurich concludes that a simple swap to 'what' questions helps us 'stay objective, future-focused, and empowered to act on our new insights'.[9]

PRINCIPLE 2: OWNERSHIP

Nearly all your coach yourself questions will have an I/my/me in them. This is because the priority is to focus on actions within our control. For example, asking, 'What is going wrong in that meeting?' results in insights we might not be able to influence, whereas asking, 'What could I do differently to make that meeting better?' makes it easier to identify what action to take.

Use I/my/me in coach yourself questions

EXAMPLES OF 'OWNERSHIP' COACH YOURSELF QUESTIONS

What action could I take?
What was my reaction?
Who could help me?

PRINCIPLE 3: IN THE MOMENT

To learn as you go, you need questions that help you to look for the learning quickly. You can do this by keeping the time frame of your questions short and by adding limitations.

Time frames: today, tomorrow, this week, next week
Limitations: one action, the most, the easiest, the quickest

EXAMPLES OF 'IN THE MOMENT' COACH YOURSELF QUESTIONS

What's one action I could take tomorrow?
What's the most important priority for me this week?
What's the easiest way for me to increase my impact next week?

How to Use Coach Yourself Questions: Pairing Awareness and Action

Pairing coach yourself questions means we can combine awareness with action that leads to learning. If we have awareness but don't act, nothing changes. If we act without awareness, we might make the wrong change. The other advantage of bringing together awareness and action is that it prompts us to reflect on past experiences and identify actions we can take in the present. This feels more motivating as we can't change the past, but we can learn from it, and choose what to do now and next.

'Reflection gives the brain an opportunity to pause amidst the chaos, untangle and sort through observations and experiences, consider multiple possible interpretations, and create meaning. This meaning becomes learning, which can then inform future mindsets and actions.'
Jennifer Porter

COACH YOURSELF QUESTION PAIRS

- **Awareness:** *What's one thing I did well today?*
- **Action:** *What's one way I could be even better tomorrow?*

Questions That Uncover Learning

- **Awareness:** *What three words would I use to describe my relationship with my manager?*
- **Action:** *When would be a good moment to ask my manager for feedback?*

- **Awareness:** *When have I had the most energy this week?*
- **Action:** *What's one change I could try to increase my energy next week?*

- **Awareness:** *What did I find frustrating today?*
- **Action:** *What will help me stay calm next time I'm in this situation?*

- **Awareness:** *What impact do I want to have in my most important meeting today?*
- **Action:** *Who could tell me which of my strengths stood out in that meeting?*

- **Awareness:** *What's top of my worry list right now?*
- **Action:** *What could help me make progress on this worry in a useful way?*

- **Awareness:** *What did I avoid doing today?*
- **Action:** *What's the first action I want to take tomorrow?*

- **Awareness:** *Who did I help today?*
- **Action:** *Who needs my support tomorrow?*

When to Add Coach Yourself Questions into Your Day

Working out when to ask and answer a coach yourself question makes it easier to start learning. Transitions can offer a useful time for reflection, as we all have these points in our day when we're going between meetings or locations. With some planning, we can turn this time into a new learning moment in our day – for example, if you have the questions saved on your phone, you won't have to search for them in the moment.

TRANSITION TIMES

- Use half of your commute to reflect on a coach yourself question.
- Use the time it takes to walk to and from a coffee shop as a chance to reflect.
- Message a friend a coach yourself question at the end of a week, and share your reflections with each other.

Situational Questions

In tricky situations, we might feel stuck or unsure about what to do. Questions can support us to learn in a way that means we can move forward. Maybe you're in a meeting and experience a sense of déjà vu as a conversation you've had before gets repeated. Or you might dread a conversation you need to have, as your relationship with that person is feeling difficult. A tricky situation needs someone to take the lead. This doesn't need to be a 'leader' by title; it can be someone who senses a situation isn't working, and has the confidence to ask different kinds of questions.

EXPERT INSIGHT: HOW CLUMSY, SNEAKY OR ATTACK QUESTIONS SHUT DOWN LEARNING

In his book ASK Jeff Wetzler observes that our question repertoire is pretty narrow compared to the range of situations we find ourselves in. He refers to a poll of two hundred executives, which found that only 15 to 25 per cent of interactions included 'real' questions.

Instead of asking quality questions – ones that 'help us learn something important from the person we ask' – Wetzler shares that we're more likely to ask clumsy, sneaky or attack questions that shut down learning rather than inviting it.

> Clumsy question: these questions close down inquiry and might sound more like statements or rhetorical: *We should progress with this project, right?*
>
> Sneaky question: these questions are designed to influence, convince or even manipulate. They feel like leading questions: *Wouldn't you agree that we should progress with this project?*
>
> Attack question: these questions put other people on the defensive. 'Why' questions often feel like attack questions, whether intended or not: *Why did you think it was a good idea to progress with this project?*
>
> 🔊 Learn more by listening to episode 216 of the *Squiggly Careers* podcast: *How to ask better questions*.

By adapting the questions you ask to the situation you're in, you can take the lead, learn more from the moment and make progress.

When/Then Questions

When/then is a short cut to quickly consider: *What question will help me learn the most in this moment?* This will prompt you to be more deliberate about choosing which questions to ask, rather than asking without thinking. To show how this works in practice we've chosen three common situations at work and shared examples of When/then questions you could ask.

> When I'm going round in circles
> Then ask questions so I can move forward and make progress

> When I'm finding it hard to work with someone
> Then ask questions so I can understand what's important to them

> When I'm being pulled in different directions
> Then ask questions so I can prioritize effectively

'I'M GOING ROUND IN CIRCLES'

This can look like repeated conversations or returning to issues that you thought had already been addressed. By highlighting rather than hiding the challenge, it shows you've spotted that something different is needed in order to make progress. This will stop you wasting time, hoping in vain that the situation will resolve itself, and will support you to be proactive in finding a solution to break the unhelpful cycle you've spotted.

When you're going round in circles
Then ask these questions:
- *Who could give me a different perspective on this challenge?*
- *What's stopping us from resolving this issue?*
- *How else could we approach the problem we want to solve?*

EXPERT INSIGHT:
MATCHING QUESTIONS WITH GOALS

In their *Harvard Business Review* article 'Relearning the art of asking questions' Tom Pohlmann and Neethi Mary Thomas recommend asking different kinds of questions depending on the goal we want to achieve.

Goal: to check understanding of a problem
Clarifying questions: to better understand what's been said

Example: *What would and wouldn't be included in the scope of solving this problem?*

Goal: to take a wide view of a problem
Adjoining questions: explore related aspects to the area being discussed

Example: *How would this impact another team or country?*

Goal: to discover something new about a problem
Funnelling questions: used to dive deeper and get to the root causes of problems

>   Example: *How did we approach this analysis?*

Goal: to explore beyond the direct problem
Elevating questions: raise broader issues and highlight the bigger picture

>   Example: *How does this connect to the purpose of the project?*

'I'M FINDING IT HARD TO WORK WITH THIS PERSON/TEAM'

This might be friction caused by competing objectives between teams or different styles of working between you and another colleague. This could be visible friction where people are sharing their disagreements openly, or hidden friction that's felt but not said. Rather than seeing friction as failure, we can ask questions to learn more about what matters to other people. Choosing to prioritize understanding and learning over winning an argument means we can be intrigued rather than intimidated by our differences.

When you're experiencing friction
Then ask these questions:
- *How do you feel about our progress on this project?*
- *What's one change you would make to this task or process?*
- *What's important to you about how we approach this?*

EXPERT INSIGHT:
EXTEND YOUR PERSONAL EMPATHY QUOTA

> 'Empathy is the art of stepping imaginatively into the shoes of another person, understanding their feelings and perspectives and using that understanding to guide your actions.' ROMAN KRZNARIC

Philosopher and author of *Empathy* Roman Krznaric shares that as adults we all have the ability to continually develop our empathetic ability by making a conscious effort to focus on the mindset of others. This can be as simple as imagining a day in the life of someone else. Krznaric encouraged people to move beyond imagining when he created the Empathy Museum in London. Visitors were asked to physically put on someone else's shoes and walk for a mile while listening to a stranger's story in their headphones. This is an example of what Krznaric describes as an 'experiential adventure'. At work this could look like shadowing someone from a different team for a day, or volunteering to complete a task on behalf of another team member to get a feel for the reality of their role.

🔊 Learn more by listening to Sarah in conversation with Roman Krznaric on episode 177 of the *Squiggly Careers* podcast.

'I'M BEING PULLED IN DIFFERENT DIRECTIONS'

This might be because you're working across different projects and priorities which all seem simultaneously urgent. Your manager is asking you to focus on one task at the same time as a senior stakeholder is demanding your attention elsewhere. This can happen because of cross-functional work, or because there's too much to get done and not enough people to make it happen. In these moments we're left feeling that we're not doing our best work anywhere. By asking questions you're not outsourcing the problem to other people; rather you're involving them in finding a solution. You demonstrate that you care about doing your work well and don't want to jeopardize important delivery. If you have a good leader, they'll also spot that these questions mean they need to lend their support to you too.

When you're being pulled in different directions
Then ask these questions:
- *If you were me, where would you start?*
- *Where will we get most return from our efforts and energy right now?*
- *Who could support us to make progress on this project and reduce the risk of missing our deadlines?*

EXPERT INSIGHT: RETIRING THE PHRASE 'DON'T BRING ME PROBLEMS, BRING ME SOLUTIONS'

CEO coach Sabina Nawaz suggests it's time to retire the phrase 'don't bring me problems, bring me solutions', as this creates a culture of fear and prevents problems from surfacing early enough. She suggests an alternative approach: when employees are involved in problem solving, it increases empowerment and the speed of resolving issues.[10]

Psychologist Adam Grant also shares that solution-only thinking creates a culture of advocacy rather than one of inquiry. This means people can approach a situation with a fixed view of the 'right' solution rather than considering multiple possibilities.

Conversational Questions

Every conversation we have at work is an opportunity to learn. Whether it's a 121 with your manager or chatting with a colleague from a different team, asking questions is how we learn what's on someone's mind, what support they need, or discover new insights and information. By widening the range of questions we ask, we can increase how much we learn from the conversations we already have.

Question Range

Consider which questions you ask the most. You might be a practical person, meaning you ask lots of 'what' questions, or someone who is good at connecting the dots, so you ask 'where' questions. Without realizing it, we often ask the same kinds of questions based on our natural biases and preferences.

- **Why questions – big picture:** *why are we focusing on this priority?*

- What questions – practical: *what would you recommend?*
- How questions – progress: *how do we make this happen?*
- Who questions – people: *who else do we need to involve?*
- Where questions – perspective: *where could we look for inspiration?*
- When questions – process: *when do we need to do this by?*

Over the next week, reflect on your current question range and notice which types of questions you are most and least likely to ask. See how it feels to ask different questions in your conversations. If you're naturally 'why' orientated, try asking 'how' questions to spot practical challenges earlier. If you're good at asking 'who' questions, you could try a 'how' question to connect people with progress. Increasing your question range will widen your learning opportunities and mean you can make the most from the conversations you have at work.

EXPERT INSIGHT:
QUESTIONS INCREASE LEARNING AND LIKING

A group of researchers from Harvard (Alison Wood Brooks, Karen Huang, Michael Yeomans, Julia Minson and Francesca Gino) looked into the question patterns of thousands of conversations between people who were getting to know each other for the first time. The participants were given fifteen minutes for the conversation and told to ask lots of questions (at least nine) or alternatively to ask minimal questions (no more than four). The people who asked the most questions were better liked by their conversation partners and gained more insight into their interests. People

were also more interested to have a second conversation with the people who asked more questions. The researchers concluded that asking a lot of questions unlocks learning and improves interpersonal bonding.[11]

Question Menus

Over the next few pages, we share some question menus to bring to life a range of different questions you could try out in the conversations you already have with your manager, peers, mentors and team members. You don't need to ask every question in one conversation, just pick the questions that feel most relevant and useful for you.

QUESTION MENU: CONVERSATION WITH YOUR MANAGER

Your manager has an important perspective on your priorities and performance. They might have insights you're missing and can connect dots that are hard for you to see. By asking a range of questions you can understand what's on your manager's mind and tap into the knowledge they have.

QUESTIONS
1. 'What do you think I need to watch out for that could get in the way of achieving my objectives?'
2. 'Where do you worry that we're not making enough progress?'

3. 'What could I do that would make your life easier?'
4. 'Who do you think I could build a useful relationship with for our team?'
5. 'When do you see me have the most positive impact?'
6. 'What team or organization do you think we could learn from?'
7. 'How could I support other people in our team?'
8. 'As a team what don't we do that you think it would be useful for us to try out?'
9. 'How can I improve our way of working together?'
10. 'I'm learning this skill at the moment . . . who would you recommend I speak to who could help me learn more?'

QUESTION MENU: CONVERSATION WITH YOUR TEAM MEMBER

If you're responsible for managing people, the questions you ask will impact how much you and your team members learn from your conversations together. Your questions are an opportunity to understand how you can support someone and what might be getting in their way. By asking a range of questions you will build stronger relationships and a better connection with your team.

QUESTIONS
1. 'What's most useful for us to talk about today?'
2. 'What does making progress on your priorities look like this week?'
3. 'How can I be helpful?'
4. 'If you could wave a magic wand, what would you change?'
5. 'What's slowing you down?'

Questions That Uncover Learning

6. 'Who could I build a relationship with that would be useful for your projects?'
7. 'Where would you like to increase your influence?'
8. 'What are you finding frustrating?'
9. 'How do you think we could improve our ways of working as a team?'
10. 'What's most likely to get in the way of achieving your objectives and outcomes?'

QUESTION MENU: CONVERSATION WITH A MENTOR

Mentors have often done something that you would like to do. By asking interesting questions you can benefit from their ideas and insights in a way that's useful for your role. Being thoughtful about your questions also helps you avoid the 'nice chat' trap, where we miss the chance to make a mentoring conversation as helpful as it could be because we haven't been specific enough about what we want to learn.

QUESTIONS

1. 'What has helped you find your way through a hard moment in the past?'
2. 'What advice has been useful for you in your career?'
3. 'Who has helped you get to where you are today?'
4. 'What skills do you think are important to invest in?'
5. 'Which role have you learned the most in?'
6. 'Which leader has inspired you?'
7. 'If you could offer your younger self one piece of advice, what would it be?'
8. 'How would you approach the challenge that I'm facing?'

9. 'How do you set goals for your career?'
10. 'When do you feel most energized in the work that you do?'

QUESTION MENU: CONVERSATION WITH A PEER

Peers are people who have similar experiences to you. They are close to your context and get what's going on in your world. Peers accelerate your learning because they have a good understanding of what you need to know. Peer-to-peer relationships are powerful and can lead to lots of mutual learning.

QUESTIONS

1. 'What helps you to make progress on projects?'
2. 'When a challenge comes your way what's been useful in finding a way forward?'
3. 'Who do you go to for useful advice or perspective?'
4. 'How do you build relationships with colleagues from other teams?'
5. 'How do you influence other people to support your work?'
6. 'What are you working on that you're most interested in?'
7. 'What supports you to do your best work?'
8. 'What's one piece of advice you'd give someone joining your team?'
9. 'What skills are you learning now?'
10. 'What are you reading, watching or listening to that you'd recommend?'

What Will I Learn?

Asking different kinds of questions accelerates our curiosity.

When we're intentional about the questions we ask, we approach our conversations with curiosity. Being curious in conversations looks like prioritizing questions motivated by intrigue, interest and a desire to discover. We stop asking questions where we think we already know the answers and start asking questions driven by learning.

When we're curious, we uncover new learning that we can't realize without having a conversation. This doesn't require a radical rethink of how you approach conversations. It means practising asking different kinds of questions. Questions of yourself, so you can take actions to continually improve. Questions so that you don't stay stuck in a situation. And a range of questions so you can learn more as you go. Curiosity is a super skill for our careers and essential if we want to stay relevant in our roles. It's how we anticipate and understand changes, make connections, and stay intrigued and interested in our work.

'Curiosity is, in great and generous minds, the first passion and the last.'
Samuel Johnson

There are lots of ways to be curious in your career, but there's no simpler or easier place to start than by asking questions with the motivation to learn as you go and grow in your role.

QUESTIONS THAT UNCOVER LEARNING: SUMMARY

1. We already ask questions at work, but usually on autopilot, which means we miss out on learning. By asking questions motivated by curiosity, understanding and openness, we discover new kinds of learning.

2. Coach yourself questions like 'Where did I have the most positive impact today?' are an easy way to increase your self-awareness and identify practical actions to accelerate your learning.

3. Matching the questions you ask to the situation you're in means you can get unstuck and learn more in tricky moments. When/then is a useful short cut to identify what kinds of questions are most useful for learning. For example: '*When* I'm finding someone difficult, *then* I ask questions to understand what's important to them.'

4. Every conversation at work is an opportunity to learn. Increasing your question range will increase how much you learn from people in return. You can use our question menus to try out new questions with managers, mentors, peers and team members.

5. Asking questions motivated by learning is a simple way to be more curious. Curiosity is a career super skill and the more expert we are at asking questions, the more relevant we will be in our roles.

DIVE INTO LEARNING LIKE A LOBSTER

- Begin by: using your next commute to reflect on a coach yourself question.
- Then try: asking a new question in a 121 with your manager.

CHAPTER 3

Data for Your Development

'The goal is to turn data into information, and information into insight.'

Carly Fiorina

We have access to more data about ourselves than ever before. We can track how many steps we've taken, how much time we've spent looking at our screens, and the quality of sleep we've had. Yet we rarely use data to influence our learning at work, and this means we miss opportunities to grow. Without data we don't know where we're starting from, where we've got to, or where we're going. Our learning loses momentum and motivation.

> **When we have data it creates clarity for our learning, and confidence in our progress.**

Lots of data is ready and waiting for us in our everyday work, and once we know where to look for it, we can start using it to our learning advantage.

EXAMPLES OF DATA FOR YOUR DEVELOPMENT

- **Numbers:** *how many meetings am I in each week?*
- **Scales:** *on a scale of 1-5 how impactful was I in that presentation?*
- **Ratio:** *what was my listening:talking ratio in my 121?*
- **Percentage:** *what percentage of my working week is spent using my strengths?*
- **Words:** *what three words do I want to be known for?*
- **Opinions:** *when do you see me at my best?*

> 'No matter the type of data, it needs a human to make meaning out of it.' CARISSA CARTER

Development Areas

To get started we've selected three areas where collecting data from the work that you already do will make an immediate difference to your development: strengths, listening and productivity. For each area we've suggested three different data points so you can build up a picture of where you are today. After collecting the data, we then recommend one way you can turn the insights you have gained into a practical action that will support you to learn as you go.

DATA FOR YOUR DEVELOPMENT

Development area	Data points	Insight into action
Strengths	1. Energy audit 2. What three words 3. Personal best	Job crafting

Data for Your Development

Development Area	Data Points	Insight into Action
Listening	1. Listening:talking ratio 2. Interruption audit 3. People pie charts	No-interruption meeting
Productivity	1. Speed vs space 2. Smart time 3. Sticking power	Deep work day

Strengths Data

> 'Each person's greatest room for growth is in areas of his or her greatest strength.' MARCUS BUCKINGHAM

It's easy to assume that our strengths don't need our attention, as they're the things we're already good at. But de-prioritizing our strengths can mean they plateau and become less useful and relevant. Just like our jobs continually change, our strengths need consistent upgrading to support our growth. Knowing, growing and showing your strengths is how you increase the impact you have in the work that you do.

There are three data points that can help you learn about your strengths:

1. Energy audit: to connect the work you enjoy with the strengths you have
2. What three words: to understand which of your strengths stand out to other people
3. Personal best: to spot ways to continually make your strengths stronger

Collecting data on your strengths will give you insights into how to increase your impact in your role today, and will mean you can pull interesting possibilities towards you for the future too.

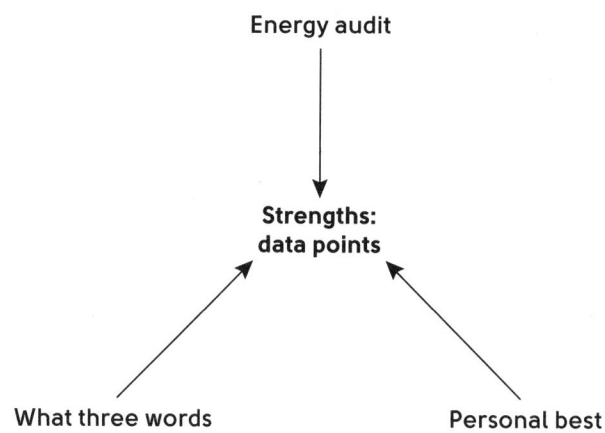

Data Point 1: Energy Audit

We all have a long list of areas we're good at, but a much shorter list of 'super strengths'. These are the distinctive strengths that we want to build a reputation for. When deciding which strengths we want to stand out, what's even more important than how good we are is how much energy and enjoyment we feel from using those strengths. By collecting data that connects our energy levels with our strengths, we can do more of the work that we find motivating and meaningful.

An energy audit helps you to spot the difference between work you are good at but find draining to do, and work you enjoy, find energizing and want to do more of.

Data for Your Development

HOW TO COLLECT DATA

Add an 'energy audit' reminder into your diary at the end of every day for two weeks.

Reflect on your day and ask yourself the same two questions:
1. When did I have the most energy today?
2. What strength(s) was I using in that moment?

Each day collect the data in a simple spreadsheet.

Once you have at least a week's worth of data, start to spot which strengths are showing up repeatedly.

EXAMPLE: ENERGY AUDIT

	When did I have the most energy today?	What strength(s) was I using?
Mon	Team meeting	Collaboration Questioning Problem solving
Tues	Working on a proposal	Creative thinking Writing Attention to detail
Weds	Client meeting	Collaboration Listening Empathy
Thurs	Coffee with colleague	Creative thinking Listening Problem solving
Fri	121 with manager	Creative problem solving

Data Point 2: What Three Words

Sometimes other people can see our strengths more clearly than we can see them for ourselves. We take our natural talents for granted and can be our own worst critic. Asking other people which of our strengths stands out to them can lead to surprising new insights for our learning.

Collecting 'what three words' data will show you which of your strengths are standing out and showing up to other people. You might have some strength blind spots, where other people can see a strength you hadn't appreciated before. Or you could discover that you're becoming known for a strength you use frequently but don't enjoy.

HOW TO COLLECT DATA

1. Write down the three words that you want to be known for.
2. Ask as many people as possible, '*What three words would you use to describe me at my best?*'
3. Once you've collected the data, compare your words with other people's words and look for where you have overlap and gaps.

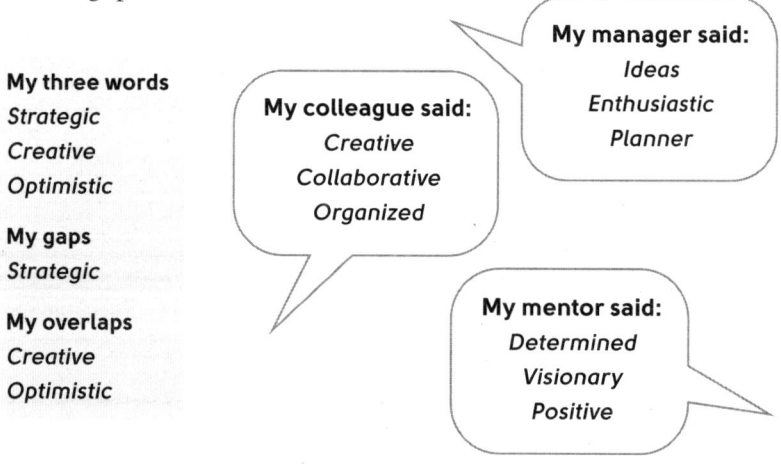

My three words
Strategic
Creative
Optimistic

My gaps
Strategic

My overlaps
Creative
Optimistic

My colleague said:
Creative
Collaborative
Organized

My manager said:
Ideas
Enthusiastic
Planner

My mentor said:
Determined
Visionary
Positive

Data Point 3: Personal Best

Our own perception of how good we are at something is often skewed by the comparisons we make with other people and their abilities. We might think we're good at presenting, until we compare ourselves to a colleague, at which point we might give up on growing in that area.

> **Comparison constrains learning.**

By collecting data on our own performance, we can set specific aims that are personal to us. Instead of competing, or comparing ourselves to others, we run our own race. Making progress on your strengths won't be a straight line process. There will be times when your data shows you're going backwards, or your performance has stalled. What matters most is that you're using the data to keep learning. To learn what works and what doesn't, to be patient and persist. Considering our personal bests also prompts us to keep developing our strengths and not become complacent with where we are right now.

HOW TO COLLECT DATA

1. Choose a strength you want to focus on, for example: *presenting*.
2. Use data to establish your current personal best, for example: *average presenting score of 6/10 based on anonymous feedback from workshop attendees.*
3. Decide on your personal best ambition, for example: *average presenting score of 8/10.*
4. Use a graph to create a visual track of your progress over time.

5. As you progress, notice what actions impact your score going up and down.

EXAMPLE OF A PERSONAL BEST LINE GRAPH

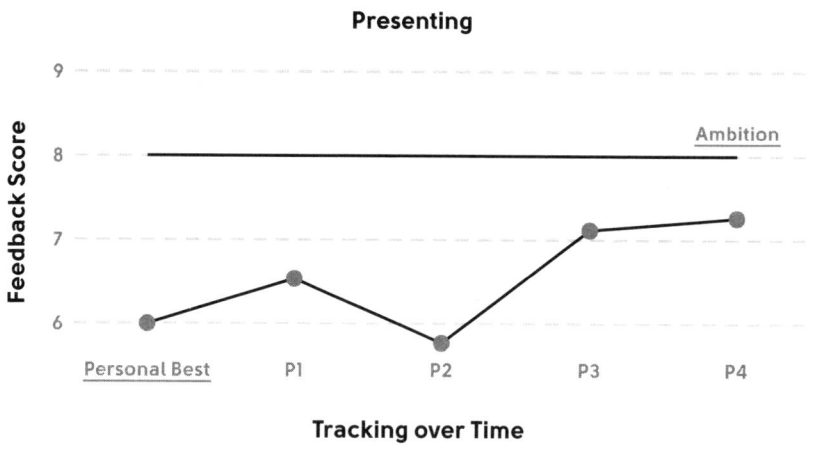

Insight into Action: Job Crafting

Your strengths insights are a useful prompt for job crafting, a process described by London Business School professor Dan Cable as 'taking the initiative to personalize your current role'. We're all used to the responsibilities in our roles changing frequently, but this usually happens *to* us rather than *with* us or being *led by* us. As Cable's research shows, job crafting works best when we connect the work we do to our distinctive strengths.

You can craft your job in small or

'The person you're competing against is your past self, and the bar you're raising is for your future self.'

Adam Grant

more significant ways. Small actions are often within your immediate control, you don't need to ask or include other people as part of the process. More significant crafting actions are usually agreed with your manager, as they impact your day-to-day responsibilities and might have implications for other people across the team.

EXAMPLES OF SMALL JOB-CRAFTING ACTIONS

- **Sharing:** host a strengths 'lunch and learn' with your team or a different department.

- **Rituals:** create weekly ways to share your strengths with other people, e.g. *a newsletter.*

- **Strengths twinning:** find a colleague who shares a strength with you, and find ways to learn from each other.

- **Outside-in:** attend external events or join outside communities focused on a strength you want to invest in.

EXAMPLES OF SIGNIFICANT JOB-CRAFTING ACTIONS

- **Deputize:** volunteer to lead a project instead of your manager, to stretch a strength. You might even work with your manager to gradually hand over the project so it can become part of your day-to-day responsibilities.

- **Responsibility swap:** swap something you're responsible for with someone else in your team. This gives you and your colleague the chance to increase how often you're using a strength you want to stretch. For example, you could swap your responsibility for designing team days with someone who wants to build on their strength of people development. In return you might take on responsibility for facilitating some of their workshops, to build your strength of creative thinking.

- **Stop: start: continue:** review your current responsibilities with the objective of using your strengths more. What would you like to stop doing, start doing and continue doing? This framework is a useful prompt for a conversation with your manager about re-crafting your role. It's unlikely you'll be able to change everything to align exactly with your strengths straight away, but this will help you to spot quick wins and opportunities to work towards.

Strengths job crafting works for everyone. You get the opportunity to make greater use of the strengths you want to be known for in your role, and your team and organization benefit from you adding more value in return.

> **EXPERT INSIGHT:**
> **CROSS-TRAINING FOR YOUR STRENGTHS**
>
> A study by researchers John Zenger, Joseph Folkman and Scott Edinger found that leaders can make their strengths stronger, not by doing more of the same, but through the development of complementary skills. For example, a leader strong in innovation could build their skill of championing change, and as a result become even more innovative in their approach. The researchers liken this to cross-training, where combining activities produces an improvement greater than we can achieve by focusing on one area alone. This 'interaction effect' can make the difference between being a good leader and an outstanding one.

Listening Data

> 'When we listen, we learn, we absorb like a sponge and are so much better because of it.'
> STEVEN SPIELBERG

Listening is a skill where we often overestimate our capability. We think we're listening, but really we're waiting to speak, assuming we know the answer, or we're preoccupied by something else that's on our mind. The average time spent listening in a conversation is just 11 seconds.[12] When we listen, we learn, and collecting data on our listening gives us visibility on how much we're learning from other people as part of our week.

Listening intently and intentionally is an opportunity for anyone who wants to learn more at work.

When we listen, it leads to understanding.

Listening intently increases the quality of our relationships and the level of influence we have with the people we work with. The more influence we have, the more ripples it makes, creating opportunities to grow in our roles. People will notice that you don't jump to conclusions but first listen to their perspective. Your colleagues will trust that you'll give them space to contribute and share their ideas. The simple act of listening can have a significant pay-off for our growth.

We'll explore three ideas to collect data and learn about your listening at work:

1. **Listening:talking ratio:** to identify how much space you give other people to share
2. **Interruption audit:** to see where you limit your learning by interrupting others
3. **People pie charts:** to understand who you're listening to and learning from

When you start to use your own data and insights to increase your listening, you'll automatically start learning more from the people you spend time with each week at work.

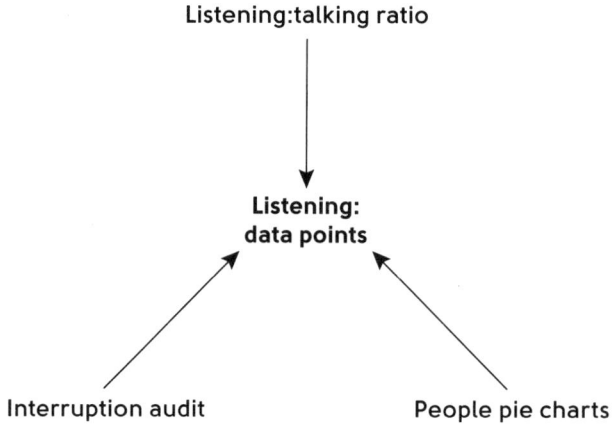

Data Point 1: Listening:Talking Ratio

This data point will give you the facts about how much time you spend listening versus talking in conversations. Listening creates space for other people to contribute, and hearing their thoughts, ideas and challenges leads to insights that help you to learn more.

When you start collecting listening data, you will begin to consider what the most useful listening:talking ratio is for you across

Data for Your Development

different conversations. For most of us there are very few conversations where we wouldn't benefit from listening more so we can learn more.

HOW TO COLLECT DATA

1. Choose a regular meeting you have with one other person or a small group.
2. Use software like Fireflies to listen into your conversation and capture the data for you (this works best for online meetings).
3. Use the data you collect to create a benchmark to improve your listening:talking ratio, and continue to track for a minimum of four meetings.

121 WITH TEAM MEMBER

	Listening	Talking
Meeting 1	20%	80%
Meeting 2	30%	70%
Meeting 3	35%	65%
Meeting 4	40%	60%

EXPERT INSIGHT: IMPROV TO IMPROVE

> 'To be a good listener is to accept pauses and silences because filling them too soon, much less pre-emptively, prevents the speaker from communicating what they are perhaps struggling to say.'
> **KATE MURPHY**

Hearing is not the same as listening. As Kate Murphy, author of *You're Not Listening*, points out, effective listening is active. The goal of the most brilliant listeners is understanding, and this takes effort. Our brains have to work hard to process incoming information. Murphy highlights that one of the more interesting and effective methods for improving employees' listening skills is improvisational drama. Improv relies on careful listening so we can pick up on the threads of what's been said before us. It requires us to be fully present and in the moment. Murphy, who took an improv class herself as part of the research for her book, concludes that 'intimacy, innovative thinking, teamwork, and humour all come to those who free themselves from the need to control the narrative and have the patience and confidence to follow the story wherever it leads'.

🔊 Learn more by listening to Kate Murphy in conversation with Helen on episode 319 of the *Squiggly Careers* podcast.

Data Point 2: Interruption Tally

> 'Interruption is a statement that the other person talking does not matter as much as we do. It harms.'
> **NANCY KLINE**

We interrupt and get interrupted for lots of different reasons. It might be to show support, because we have an idea to share, to disagree with a point being made, or to speed up a conversation where we've already decided what needs to get done. However, the moment we interrupt someone's flow we lose out on an opportunity to learn.

Collecting data on interruptions will give you two insights: how frequently you interrupt, and the reason for your interruptions. These insights can prompt new actions that offer an alternative to interrupting. Rather than say an idea in the moment, you might write it down to share later. Rather than speak up to support, you might nod your head and smile in encouragement.

The best way to learn from someone is to give them space to speak.

HOW TO COLLECT DATA

1. Pick a partner: collecting this data works best if you partner with someone you work with regularly and trust.
2. Ask them to choose at least one meeting you're in together over the next month (but it's important they don't tell you which meeting).
3. Your partner uses a blank version of the table below to mark down how often you interrupt and the reasons for your interruptions. You could offer to do the same process in return the following month.
4. Ask your partner to repeat the process in a month's time to see if you've managed to reduce the frequency of your interruptions.

INTERRUPTION AUDIT

Total interruptions	||||| ||||| = 10
Reason for interruption	
Interrupt to support	II
Interrupt with an idea	IIII
Interrupt to disagree	
Interrupt to ask a question	IIII
Interrupt to speed up	
Other	

Data Point 3: People Pie Charts

If we always listen to the same people, even if they are brilliant, we risk getting stuck in an echo chamber and limiting our learning. This is an easy trap to fall into, as our roles typically mean we spend time with lots of the same people each week.

Collecting data on the diversity of your conversations will give you insights into how much 'sameness' you have across your current connections. If we stick to conversations in our siloes, with people we've met before, we're more likely to be reinforcing what we already know rather than learning something new. This data can prompt us to increase the range of people we spend time with as part of our role.

EXPERT INSIGHT:
THE POWER OF COGNITIVE DIVERSITY

In his book *Rebel Ideas* Matthew Syed describes how we all have models and heuristics (short cuts for our brain) that we instinctively use to make sense of the world. The challenge is that we unconsciously spend time with people who have the same or similar models to ourselves, and consequently limit our learning. Cognitive diversity is achieved by spending time with people who think in different ways, offer alternative perspectives, and have a variety of information processing styles.

> 'The path to wisdom is not to surround ourselves with people who think the same, but to connect with those who think differently.'
> Matthew Syed

🔊 Learn more by listening to Matthew Syed in conversation with Helen on episode 139 of the *Squiggly Careers* podcast.

HOW TO COLLECT DATA

For your next ten conversations track who you are talking to and capture data on four areas:

1. person you've met before or new connection
2. person in your team or person outside your team
3. person in your organization or person outside your organization
4. person connected to your day job or person connected to your development

EXAMPLES OF PEOPLE PIE CHARTS FOR LAST 10 CONVERSATIONS

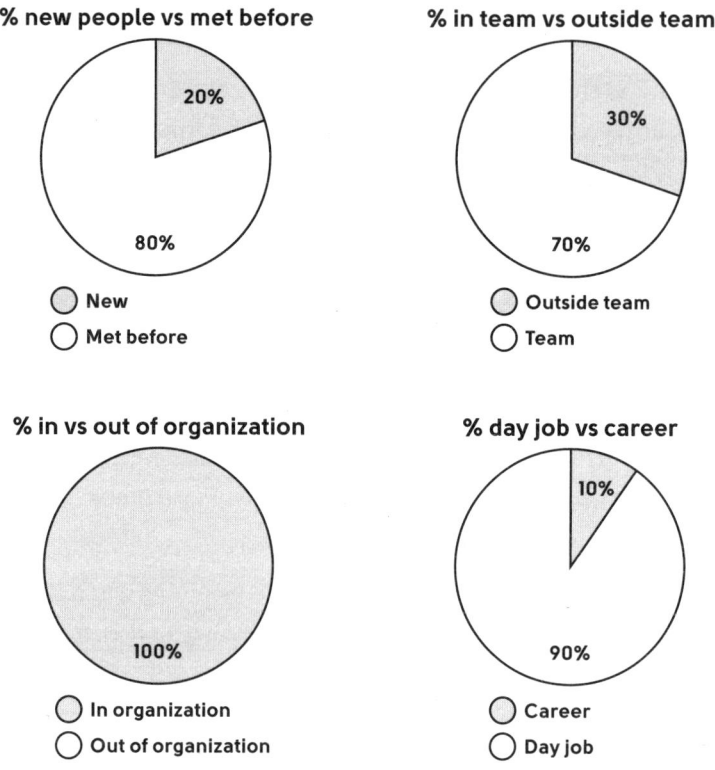

Insight Into Action: No-Interruption Meetings

Nancy Kline, author of *Time to Think*, shares that when someone commits to not interrupting us, we feel relief, enjoy more space to think, are braver about sharing our thoughts, and receive permission to be ourselves.[13] These are big benefits both for us and the people around us. Telling a person or a group of people that we're going to work hard to not interrupt may feel out of the ordinary – and even a bit uncomfortable to say out loud – but you might be surprised about what you learn in return. Channelling all our focus into listening means we stop guessing what someone might say or worrying about how we're going to respond.

Step 1: choose a no-interruption moment or meeting

Look at your week and identify a meeting or moment where you'd like to learn more. Maybe you want to get a better understanding of how your team is feeling, so the focus would be your 121 conversations. Or you want to learn more about different parts of your organization, so it's a cross-functional project meeting.

Step 2: switch saying for writing

One of the reasons we interrupt is a desire to share the thoughts that pop into our head immediately. This is driven by enthusiasm for the idea or perhaps a concern that if we don't talk straight away, we'll forget an important point. When these thoughts occur during a no-interruption meeting, practise writing them down. That way, you don't get distracted by trying to remember them and you don't interrupt either. You might find that, by leaving space for other people, they share the same or an even better point anyway.

Step 3: ask don't assume

Sometimes we make the mistake of equating adding value with talking, i.e. the people who talk the most, know the most. This can mean that when we switch to listening more and talking less in conversations, we come away concerned that we haven't been useful or helpful for other people. To challenge this assumption, ask people to share their experience of a no-interruption meeting with you. Hearing the positive impact of no interruptions firsthand from the people we work with can give us the reassurance to keep going.

It's unlikely you'll eliminate all interruptions from your conversations, but by reducing how often you interrupt you'll be rewarded with more learning in your role, and better relationships with your colleagues too.

Productivity Data

> **'I didn't get there by wishing for it or hoping for it, but by working for it.'** ATTRIBUTED TO ESTÉE LAUDER

Productivity, in simple terms, is the amount of work we can get done in a day. We're all drawn to the idea of being more productive, spending our time at work well and fitting more into our minutes. We might feel in equal parts inspired and intimidated when we read about successful CEOs and high-flying founders who get up at 5 a.m. to read, run and meditate before they even begin their workday. The pressure to be productive and optimize every part of our day can mean we feel we have to make a trade-off between *learning* more or *doing* more.

Collecting data on your patterns of productivity means you can start making more conscious choices about how you spend your time at work. You will spot ways to make sure that your time at work is well spent and that you're working in a way that increases the chances of being successful in your role.

In this section we share three activities to collect data on your productivity:

1. **Speed vs space:** to understand whether the pace of your day is working for or against you
2. **Smart time:** to see whether notifications are taking up time when you could be learning
3. **Sticking power:** to identify how long you can stick with doing one task uninterrupted

When you start to use your own data and insights to impact your productivity, you can make decisions about doing work in a way that will increase how much you can achieve and learn every day.

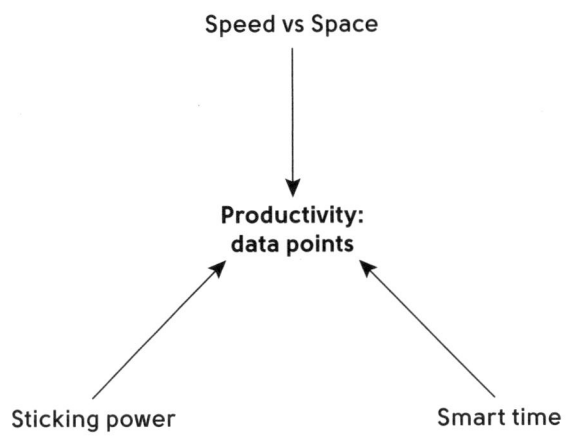

Data Point 1: Speed vs Space

> **'Without a pause, everything continues as it was.'**
> ROBERT POYNTON

Spending our days at top speed gets in the way of learning. We become blinkered and burnt out and somehow feel like we're achieving less than ever. Slowing down doesn't need to be a dramatic change to your day; it's more likely to look like punctuating your day with short pauses. Slowing down is an important part of what it takes to be productive. It can look like taking a break before completing a presentation so you can spot mistakes you might have missed. It can mean taking a short pause before an important meeting to consider ahead of time the questions you want to ask. Varying your pace at work opens up opportunities to learn that pass us by if we always feel like we're sprinting from one thing to the next.

This idea for collecting data is borrowed with the kind permission of Robert Poynton, author of *Do / Pause*. By plotting out your pace you will get quick visual data on how much speed and space you have in your work today.

HOW TO COLLECT DATA

1. Have a look back at your diary for yesterday.
2. Use the letter I to represent speed and the letter O to represent space.
3. Plot your pace during your day by applying the Is and Os to your time, and see what you notice.

Here are contrasting examples of two people experiencing very different days.

Person 1: OOIIIIIIIIIIIIIIIIIIIIIIIIIIOO – the only space in the day is the commute.

Person 1 has lots of back-to-back meetings and feels like they're constantly switching between emails, messages and meetings. This person is likely to make more mistakes as the day goes on and be drained by the time they finish work. This person describes their day as 'always on' and 'frantic'.

Person 2: OOIIIIOOIIIOOIIIIOIIIIOO – regular moments of space in the day.

Person 2 has regular short moments of space in their day. This might look like taking the time to have a coffee with a colleague or taking ten minutes to think before an important meeting. They're more likely to do high-quality work, and they have capacity to learn along the way. This person describes their day as 'energizing' and 'interesting'.

Data Point 2: Smart Time

Our smartphones are in danger of making us less smart. While we might be more connected to everything and everyone in our world, constant alerts, notifications and device-led distractions take away from time that we could be investing in our learning.

Our relationships with our phones have changed over time. No one makes a conscious choice to pick their phone up every hour, to spend two hours a day scrolling, or to look at it every time a message appears. While a smartphone provides flexibility in how and where we do our work, it can also lead to wasting time and feeling frustrated about unproductive patterns of behaviour.

Collecting data on the number of notifications you receive in a day is a simple way to start noticing whether you are using your phone in a way that makes you more or less productive. Every notification we turn off becomes an opportunity to turn more learning on. For example, if you receive 100 notifications a day, and each notification takes up 30 seconds of your time, turning them all off would give you 50 minutes more time in a day. Turning even half of your notifications off would mean you had nearly half an hour that could become 'new' learning time. This could be your time to try out an everyday experiment, or ask a coach yourself question, or start collecting some extra data for your development.

HOW TO COLLECT DATA

1. Use the screen time function in your phone to look at the number of notifications you receive.
2. Write down your top five sources of notifications (e.g. WhatsApp) and the number of notifications for each application.
3. Over a week, turn off the notification function for each app (one app a day).
4. Reflect on the total number of notifications you are now receiving, and whether you are feeling more or less productive.

EXAMPLE

Helen and Sarah spontaneously compared the daily number of notifications they received. Prompted by the big difference between their data, Helen learned from Sarah's approach and turned off her non-essential notifications. It's still much higher than Sarah's daily average, but it's now coming in at a slightly more manageable 100–150 per day. As a result, Helen feels less pressured to pick up her phone to respond, and more able to stay focused on what she is working on.

Data for Your Development

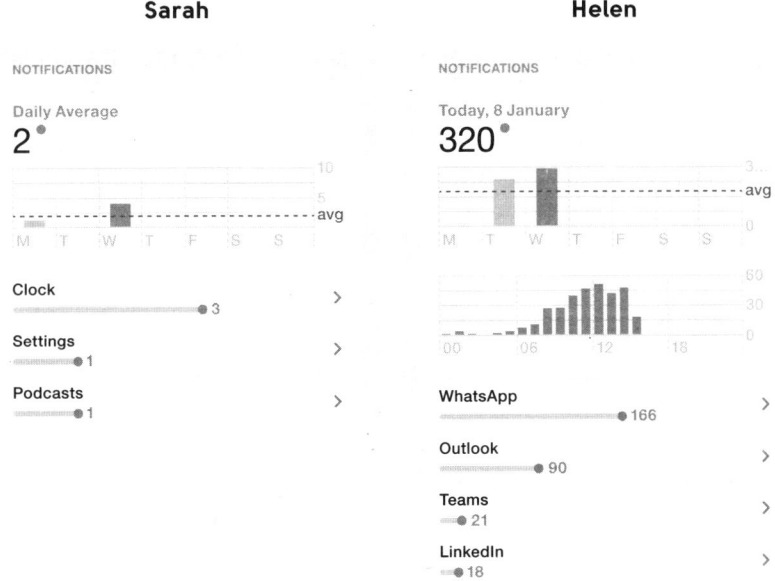

EXPERT INSIGHT:
HOW TO BREAK UP WITH YOUR PHONE

Catherine Price, author of *How to Break Up with Your Phone*, outlines how our brains are designed to keep us glued, even addicted, to our phones. Our phones have a lot in common with slot machines, one of the most addictive devices ever to be invented. Like the slot machine a phone offers us occasional, intermittent rewards, and this is enough to keep us coming back for more. Our phones light up all the reward centres of our brains, so much so that we often get a dopamine hit *before* we even pick up our phone.

Phones also offer us endless novelty and distraction, again something our brains crave. Price points out that one of the downsides for our brains is the impact our phones have on our short-term, or working, memory. She describes how our smartphones provide us with a 'virtual avalanche of information', leaving little space for anything else and impacting our capacity for insights, ideas and deep thought. The evidence is overwhelming: if we want to learn more from our days, we need to spend less time on our phones.

Data Point 3: Sticking Power

When you've got a lot to do, switching between tasks can feel like the fastest way to move things forward. Moving from writing a presentation, to running a meeting, to sending an email, and then calling a client might feel efficient but it's not effective for learning. The more we switch, the less we learn. When *everything* feels important and urgent, we're less able to make informed decisions about our work and learn from what we're doing. We respond to every ask and distraction that comes our way, and struggle to give our complete attention to any one task.

Collecting data on the length of time you can stick to one task will increase your awareness of how easy or hard you find it to pay attention, and give you insights into your concentration span.

HOW TO COLLECT DATA

1. Identify thirty minutes a day when you have freedom over how you spend your time.
2. Choose a task that needs your attention.
3. Set a stopwatch and get started.
4. Record how long you can stick to a single task without getting distracted or multi-tasking.

5. Continue to collect this data for two weeks, to see what happens. The aim is for your concentration span to increase during this period.

STICKING POWER

Week 1	Monday	Tuesday	Wednesday	Thursday	Friday
	10 minutes	15 minutes	10 minutes	20 minutes	30 minutes
Week 2	Monday	Tuesday	Wednesday	Thursday	Friday
	10 minutes	25 minutes	20 minutes	30 minutes	30 minutes

EXPERT INSIGHT: THE COST OF SWITCHING

Dr Gloria Mark, a professor of informatics at the University of California, leads research on how our attention span affects our lives.[14] None of the numbers are heading in the right direction:

- In 2004 average attention on a screen was 2½ minutes; now it's 47 seconds.
- When we switch our attention, it takes 25 minutes and 26 seconds before we go back to the original project.
- We don't just switch between Project A and Project B; in fact, we're more likely to go from Project A to Project B, to Project C and even D, before returning back to A again.

A reduced attention span is not an irreversible state; there are simple actions we can take that make a difference. For example, Mark shares that attention is goal-directed and we're better at staying on task if we regularly remind ourselves of what we want to achieve. This can be as simple as writing your goal on a Post-it note that you can see, or sharing your single most important priority with your team at the start of a week.

Insight Into Action: Deep Work Day

> 'Being busy is not the same as being productive. True productivity is about achieving meaningful goals, and that often requires slowing down.'
> **CAL NEWPORT**

Cal Newport, author of *Slow Productivity*, suggests that people are busy being 'pseudo-productive' at work, where they appear to be busy but aren't actually engaging in meaningful or high-value work. This kind of busy work creates a false sense of accomplishment and doesn't significantly contribute to long-term success. Newport recommends slowing down and doing fewer things in a day.

You might feel out of practice with what slowing down looks like, or feel daunted by the prospect if you're someone who enjoys working at a fast pace. Using the insights you get from collecting data on your productivity to design a one-off deep work day is a good place to start.

Step 1: Look a month ahead in your diary and identify a day where you can block out time to work on one or two high-priority actions. These should be actions that require a few hours of sustained effort from you to progress or, even better, complete.

Step 2: Set your day up for productivity. Think about your preferred location, what time your day will start and finish, how frequently you'll need breaks, and any tech or notifications that you'll need to turn off in order to focus.

Step 3: Share your planned deep work day with relevant team members, so they understand what you are doing and can minimize asks and interruptions during the day.

Step 4: After your deep work day, reflect on how productive you felt. Write down a list of three things to 'do again' and three to 'do differently' if you were to design a similar day again.

What's most important about a deep work day is not trying to magic-up lots of days with zero distractions, but applying the insights you learn back into your every day. Maybe you spotted you had the best ideas when you went for a short walk, and that's something you can keep doing. Or you realize that your notifications aren't needed and you can switch at least some of them off.

What Will I Learn?

> **Collecting data for your development leads to better decision making.**

Data helps us to make better decisions. Decisions that are informed by a range of data points tell us a story about how much we're learning. Data by itself doesn't give us answers but it prompts us to look for insights into where we're doing well and what gaps need our attention.

If we want our data to change, we need to make different decisions. These are not necessarily big decisions, but small decisions about our development and how we do our jobs. A decision to listen more by limiting interruptions in 121 conversations. A decision to slow down for fifteen minutes, because you know it'll speed up your thinking in an important meeting later. A decision to ask two of your colleagues for feedback on your strengths, to see where you're having a positive impact. These small decisions are decisions to learn. A decision to be lobster-like and make the most of the data that's available to support your development and stay relevant in your role.

DATA FOR YOUR DEVELOPMENT: SUMMARY

1. We use data to inform lots of parts of our lives but rarely collect data to influence our development. Data tells us a story about how much we're learning, it shows us where we're starting from and supports us to track our progress.

2. It's easy to assume that our strengths don't need our attention, but this is where we have the most opportunity to grow. Collecting data on what gives you energy, the strengths that other people see in you, and tracking your personal best performance will give you insights into how to increase your impact.

3. How much you're listening is an insight into how much you're learning. By collecting data on who we listen to and how well we listen, we can spot ways to learn more from the people we work with.

Data for Your Development

4. We all want to make sure that our time at work is well spent. Collecting data on your pace, distractions and attention span will support you to assess your productivity and spot ways to achieve more at work.

5. Data gives us insights into how to make better decisions for our development. We can all make the decision to be lobster-like with our learning, so we don't miss out on opportunities to learn as we go.

DIVE INTO LEARNING LIKE A LOBSTER
- Begin by: completing an energy audit over the next week.
- Then try: measuring your listening:talking ratio in a meeting.

Part 2

Learn in Hard Moments

*'Sometimes there's not a better way.
Sometimes there's only a hard way.'*

Mary E. Pearson

A lobster's growth happens automatically, but not easily. As a lobster gets bigger its shell starts to feel uncomfortable and constraining, signalling the start of a process called 'moulting' or *ecdysis*, the Greek word for 'getting out'. The moulting process involves the lobster absorbing water, expanding its body and pushing apart its existing shell until it comes off. This is as difficult, stressful and exhausting as it sounds and after losing the safety of its hard shell, the lobster emerges in a very different form. It has become soft, squishy and jelly-like, almost unrecognizable from the hard-shelled lobster it once was.

This is a vulnerable time for the lobster. Outside of its protective shell it's exposed and at risk of attack. But lobsters get lots of practice at finding their way through this tough time. In the first 5 to 7 years of a lobster's life, it will moult almost 25 times, and though the frequency of the moulting reduces, it never stops. As a result, lobsters have developed smart survival and risk-reducing tactics. During moulting they find cover in crevices or under rocks, to decrease the chances of being eaten by an opportunistic passing seal or attacked by an angry crab. The pay-off for a lifelong commitment to navigating this difficult process is that a lobster grows by around 20 per cent each time it sheds its shell.[15] The risk of vulnerability is worth the reward; by repeatedly finding its way through a hard moment, the lobster guarantees its continual growth.

Everyone has 'shell shedding' moments in their jobs and careers.

Restructures, difficult feedback, a project failing, making mistakes, challenging managers. These tough times happen to all of us and can leave us feeling a bit 'jelly-like', exactly like our friend the lobster. In the drained and depleted state that comes with these challenges, learning isn't front of mind; we just want to make it through and move on. The problem with being in 'make it through' mode is that we don't take advantage of the big leaps of learning that are available to us in these hard moments.

Growing through tough times is in a lobster's DNA, but for us it has to be a conscious decision.

We can choose whether to learn from or be limited by our experiences.

Imagine if, like the lobster, you learned 20 per cent more each time something went wrong at work. Or if asking for feedback more frequently meant you could become 30 per cent better at your job. When we learn like a lobster, it means we see challenges as a chance to grow in a new way.

Why Learning in Hard Moments Will Help You Grow

> 'Failure is an important part of your growth and developing resilience.' MICHELLE OBAMA

Challenges will always be there, but learning in hard moments leads to resilience. Being resilient doesn't mean we have to cope by ourselves or 'tough it out'. It looks like having the confidence and know-how to learn our way through knotty moments, and by being resilient we can turn a tough time into something that's helpful for our growth.

> There's no such thing as a straight line to success in our careers.

What Gets in the Way of Learning in Hard Moments

Hard moments feed our fears and grow our gremlins. Everyone has confidence gremlins, beliefs that hold us back, and these tend to show up the most when we need them the least. At a time when we need to believe in ourselves, they tell us that we're not good enough, smart enough or that we're about to be found out. An important part of learning in hard moments and staying resilient is putting gremlins in their place. It's reminding ourselves that one mistake doesn't make us a failure, or that something going wrong is rarely down to just one person.

If our gremlins weren't enough to grapple with, our egos can also get in the way. We all have an ego – it's our sense of self – and when we experience a hard moment, our ego takes a hit. An ego-led response means that, rather than reflecting on what went wrong, we're more likely to deflect, defend or blame someone else. Letting go of our ego encourages us to ask for help, admit that we don't know, and stop pretending to be perfect.

When we let go of our ego, we let learning in.

Learning like a lobster means we have the confidence to be vulnerable and to see fears and failures as not only part of the process, but one of the most valuable ways we have of learning.

How to Learn in Hard Moments

In Part 2 we focus on how you can learn during a challenging moment. If we wait for a tough time to be over and rely on looking back in order to learn, we miss out on the opportunity to grow while that hard time is happening. In our careers and jobs, we don't have lots of control over some of the difficulties that come our way, but we can control how much we learn in that moment. We can choose to see challenge as a chance to grow.

The next two chapters cover topics that are hard for everyone, where learning is most likely to get missed. First, we cover a particularly hard skill: feedback, and how to put learning first. Second, we explore how to learn when things go wrong, whether it's a small mistake or a significant failure.

CHAPTER 4

Feedback That Puts Learning First

'If we shield ourselves from feedback, we stop growing.'

Brené Brown

Do you have five minutes for some feedback? Receiving this message from our manager would probably send most of us into panic mode. We'd try to work out what we might have done wrong; our anxiety levels would be sky high, and by the time the dreaded five minutes arrive we've convinced ourselves we're going to be fired. Feedback is both an opportunity and a threat. An opportunity to learn and grow in new ways, and a threat to our identity – who we are and how we see ourselves. Our fears surrounding feedback are so significant that we choose to protect ourselves and stay in our shell over the opportunity to learn and grow.

What If? Feedback Fears

The idea of feedback raises lots of 'what if?' questions that reinforce our fears and mean we avoid action. These fears create assumptions and emotions about asking for, giving and receiving feedback that feel hard to overcome.

Asking for Feedback Fear:
'What If Feedback Makes Me Feel Worse?'

No one likes to be criticized. It can feel like we're being 'told-off' and cause our 'not good enough' doubts to creep in. The risk of adding other people's criticisms to the negative thoughts we already have about ourselves feels exposing. Criticism can damage our self-esteem and challenge our sense of worth. Academic Daniel Goleman shares that threats to our esteem are so significant that they 'can literally feel like threats to our very survival'.[16]

Giving Feedback Fear:
'What If Feedback Causes Friction or Hurts Someone's Feelings?'

We worry that some feedback might create friction or result in a challenging conversation. Conflict avoidance and the fear of disagreement often get in the way of giving feedback that could be valuable for other people. We know that we need to continue working with our colleagues constructively, so jeopardizing those relationships with feedback feels like a big risk. We're also wired for empathy, cooperation, generosity and connection.[17] When we fear that feedback might hurt someone's feelings, or even 'break up' a relationship that matters to us, it can make us question whether it's worth the effort.

Receiving Feedback Fear: 'What If I Don't Agree?'

At some point in our careers, we all receive feedback that we don't agree with. This can leave us in a difficult position about how we should respond. If the feedback is from someone senior, we might not feel comfortable to question them about the details. Or the feedback might leave us feeling pressured to take an action that doesn't feel authentic. At times our emotions might work against us, and we become visibly angry or upset about the feedback. This often results in 'receiving regrets', where we don't feel happy with how we responded in the moment.

> **Feedback works when we overcome our fears and put learning first.**

When we find ways to overcome our fears, feedback can help us to learn in a way that nothing else can. By involving other people in our learning, we gain new insights and alternative perspectives. We learn about our blind spots, and our colleagues can spot strengths in us that we might take for granted. Asking, giving and receiving feedback with a learning lens is how we start to reduce some of the fears that get in the way of our growth.

Feedback accelerates our growth in a way that we can't achieve alone.

How to Ask, Give and Receive Feedback in a Way That Puts Learning First

'Easy choices, hard life. Hard choices, easy life.'
JERZY GREGOREK

It will always be easier to not ask for or give feedback. It can also be tempting to ignore feedback that we found disappointing or confusing. But avoiding feedback limits our learning potential. In the rest of this chapter we share tried and tested techniques that make all types of feedback easier, by putting learning first.

- How to frame feedback to make it easier to ask for and quicker to receive
- How to give feedback that supports you and other people to grow
- How to use the feedback you receive to multiply your learning

FEEDBACK THAT PUTS LEARNING FIRST

Feedback skill	Actions
Asking	1. Framers 2. Advice accelerators
Giving	1. Brilliant because 2. Say the hard thing
Receiving	1. Think/feel/do 2. The multiplier effect

Asking for Feedback

Vague requests for feedback are hard for people to respond to in a way that's useful for our learning.

Vague asks sound like:

- 'Can I have some feedback when you have a spare five minutes?'
- 'What did you think of my presentation?'
- 'How do you think I'm doing?'

Framing makes your asks for feedback easier to answer by offering people some guidelines around what you'd like to know. When people know what kind of feedback you need, it speeds up the process. Framed feedback feels much less daunting to give, and the

Focus	**Plus one**
The what	*The who*

Feedback Frames
How to make feedback asks easy to answer

Quick asks	**Same day**
The how	*The when*

result is much more useful for you. There are four ways that you can start framing your feedback asks.

Frame 1: Focus

What do you want feedback on? Do you want to learn about your strengths, or are you aiming to improve a specific skill? Focusing your feedback will make your ask specific, easily understood by someone else and mean that the insights you receive are more relevant for your learning.

EXAMPLES OF FOCUS FRAMES
- **Improvement focus:** 'What's one way I could improve my writing skills?'
- **Idea focus:** 'What ideas do you have to make our meetings more efficient?'
- **Change focus:** 'What would you change about this proposal?'
- **Impact focus:** 'What was most useful about my presentation today?'
- **Advice focus:** 'What's your advice on building relationships with other teams?'

Frame 2: Plus One

A 'plus one' frame helps you to go beyond the obvious person with your ask. By asking the same feedback question to more than one person, you learn about yourself from different perspectives, which gives you a more complete view of how you are showing up at work.

It helps you to collect more information and compare and contrast people's responses.

PLUS ONE FEEDBACK

Example question	Ask 1	Plus 1
'Which three words would you use to describe me at my best?'	Manager	Peer
'What's one way I could increase my impact in our meetings together?'	Team member	Colleague from a different function
'What skill have you seen me using when we work together?'	Colleague you work with frequently	Colleague you work with occasionally
'What do you think was the most useful part of my presentation today?'	A new team member	An experienced team member

Frame 3: Quick Asks

A quick ask is an action that can be done straight away and doesn't fall into the 'I'll get to that later (or never)' file. When we make quick asks for feedback, it leads to 'little and often' learning.

EXAMPLES OF QUICK ASKS
- 'What's one word that reflects how you feel about our conversation?'
- 'What's one small change I could make to how I approach the team meeting?'
- 'What stood out the most to you from the work I shared today?'
- 'Who would you recommend I speak to so I can learn more about this area?'

Frame 4: Same-Day Feedback

We often delay asking for the feedback we need. It might be that a 'What if?' fear is holding us back, or we assume that it's better to wait for a meeting in person in a few weeks' time. However, if we wait until tomorrow or the end of the week, asking for feedback is more likely to fall off our to-do list. And if we do eventually ask, people may have forgotten what happened, resulting in patchy and inaccurate feedback. Framing our feedback asks with 'today' in mind will improve the quality of the feedback you receive.

> EXAMPLES OF SAME-DAY FEEDBACK
> - **Reminders:** add a 5-minute action into your diary after a meeting to give yourself time to quickly send an instant message to two people you'd like feedback from.
> - **Meetings and moments:** add feedback into meetings and moments that you have ownership for. For example, in your 121s with your manager you could start the conversation by asking a feedback question like: 'When do you see me having a positive impact in our team at the moment?'
> - **Feedback Thursdays:** to get started you could pick a day each week where you commit to always asking for feedback about that day. It works best to pick a day where you typically spend lots of time in meetings and collaborating with colleagues, so you have a range of people and moments to pick from each week.

EXPERT INSIGHT:
MICROSOFT'S 'BRAIN-FRIENDLY' APPROACH TO FEEDBACK

Microsoft have introduced a new 'brain-friendly' approach to feedback called the Perspectives tool. The features of the tool are designed with growth in mind, for example employees can make specific asks about the input they're looking for. This builds on research showing that we're more receptive to feedback we've asked for. Perspectives has also instigated a critical change in the flow of feedback within Microsoft. Previously, feedback had been anonymized and filtered through managers. Now feedback is delivered directly from peers, and the tool will even make suggestions on who you could ask for feedback, with the aim of widening the range of perspectives an employee can benefit from.

Advice Accelerators

The word 'feedback' often provokes negative associations and assumptions. Even if that's not the case for you, it's likely to be true for some of the people you'd like feedback from. When a word's associations get in the way of our learning, it's useful to try a different approach. Swapping the word 'feedback' for 'advice' can be a more effective way to learn from the people around us. Researchers found that feedback is often associated with evaluation of how someone performed in the past, which can lead to vague statements. However, when we're asked to give advice, our responses become significantly more useful and actionable. In one study when people were asked to offer advice, they suggested 56 per cent more ways to improve.[18] Asking for advice is one of the easiest ways to increase the value you get from feedback. The more we ask for advice, the more opportunities we create to learn.

Imagine a situation where you're trying to run a meeting so that everyone feels included. In scenario one, you ask a colleague for feedback after the meeting. In scenario two, you ask the same colleague for their advice about what you could do differently to increase everyone's engagement. Looking at the responses below helps to see the difference in learning.

SITUATION: YOU WANT TO INCREASE INCLUSION IN A MEETING YOU RUN

Scenario 1 (Feedback)	Scenario 2 (Advice)
You ask: 'I'd appreciate your feedback on how well I included everyone in our last team meeting together.'	You ask: 'I'd like to make sure everyone has a chance to contribute to our meeting. What's your advice on what I can do next time so everyone feels included?'
Response: 'I thought it was good. There are a few people who might need more of a nudge next time, but overall it was okay.'	Response: 'I'd suggest you ask people for agenda items in advance to avoid assuming what's important for people. One extra thought is you could try rotating roles in the meeting to give you the opportunity to observe the group and see if everyone is involved, without the pressure of facilitating the conversation.'
What Do You Learn?	**What Do You Learn?**
Vague and unspecific information	Actionable insight

Being clear about what you want to learn when you're asking for advice helps you to be more specific about how you ask. When people understand why you've gone to them for advice, it makes your ask more credible and helps them to feel more confident in responding to your request.

While there are no limits on who you can ask for advice, we would suggest there are four categories of people who are particularly valuable:

- **Critical friends** who can see your blind spots
- **Experts** who will make your strengths stronger
- **Outsiders** who can offer new ideas and perspectives
- **Builders** who can see how to make your work better

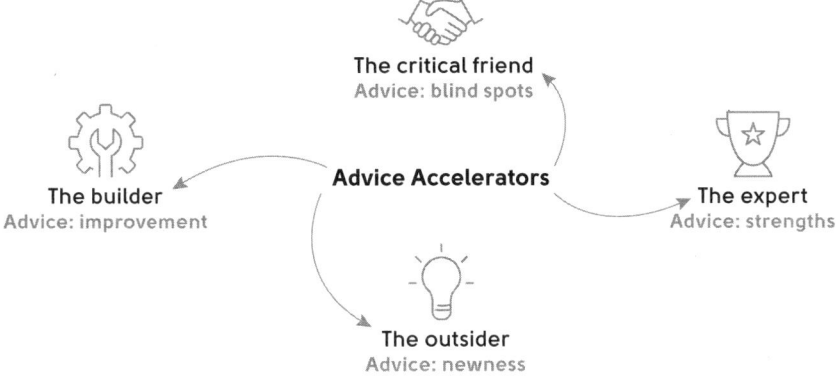

THE CRITICAL FRIEND

This is someone you trust, who is on your side and wants you to succeed. This person works with you frequently and has seen you at your brilliant best and on your worst days too. Critical friends are honest with you in ways that other people might not feel comfortable to be. They will tell you where you are getting in your own way, and offer you advice you won't hear from anyone else.

EXAMPLES OF ASKING FOR ADVICE FROM A CRITICAL FRIEND

- 'I didn't get the promotion I applied for and now feel stuck. What would you suggest I do?'
- 'I'm struggling to build a strong relationship with my manager. What do you think I'm getting wrong?'
- 'I'm not getting opportunities to work on the projects that are most exciting to me. What could I do differently?'

THE EXPERT

Experts can seem intimidating from a distance, but they didn't get to where they are overnight and that means they have a lot of useful insight. By asking for their advice, you can fast-track your learning. They can pass on their skills and expertise to you and offer advice based on what has worked well for them. You don't need to have worked directly with this person for them to be useful for your learning.

EXAMPLES OF ASKING FOR ADVICE FROM AN EXPERT

- 'I admire your storytelling skills and it's something I enjoy and would like to be known for. I wondered if you could share one storytelling technique that's worked for you that I could try out?'
- 'I enjoy working on cross-functional projects and it's something I want to do more of. I see you as a real expert in this area and I wondered what advice you'd give me so I can improve my skills?'

- 'I love leading teams and I'm working on being the best leader I can. I really relate to your leadership style and wondered if you had any advice on how to develop my leadership skills?'

THE OUTSIDER

Asking for advice from people who are outside of our day to day gives us a different perspective. Your outsiders might be people from other parts of your organization or different industries and companies. If you're in a large organization, you might look for advice from someone in a start-up environment. If you're in a business-to-business sector, you could ask for advice from someone who works in a consumer-focused organization. Outsiders help us to learn new ways of thinking and identify different ways to overcome obstacles.

EXAMPLES OF ASKING FOR ADVICE FROM AN OUTSIDER

- 'I'm finding it hard to persuade senior people to prioritize our sustainability ideas. I wondered what advice you could share based on what's worked for you?'

- 'I want to develop my copywriting skills and was thinking of starting a newsletter. I really enjoy yours and I wondered what advice you'd have based on what you've learned so far?'

- 'I'm interested in how I can create an environment where creativity thrives. I feel like your sector/organization is leading the way on this, and I'd love to learn from your experience.'

THE BUILDER

Builders can offer specific and practical advice on how you can improve. Builders tend to have first-hand experience of what we're doing and can be objective and supportive with their suggestions. It's often useful to ask a builder for advice *during* a process rather than *after* you've finished, so you can apply what you learn straight away. Builders can support you to get better in a way that's often hard to see for yourself from within a process.

EXAMPLES OF ASKING FOR ADVICE FROM A BUILDER

- 'I'd appreciate your advice on a proposal I'm putting together. How do you think I could make it more compelling?'

- 'I've started using more data in my presentations. Can I show you an example of what this looks like and get your builds and suggestions?'

- 'I'm struggling to share my research findings in an interesting way. This is how I usually present them, what advice would you give me on what I could do differently?'

WHAT TO WATCH OUT FOR

Whether you're asking for advice from an outsider, a builder, an expert or a critical friend, there are some watch-outs to keep in mind.

Watch-out 1: advice not answers – look out for mistaking advice for the 'right' answer. Advice is just one approach for you to consider; use other people's perspective to create your own answers.

Watch-out 2: advice overwhelm – asking for advice from too many people at the same time can lead to lots of different opinions and create confusion rather than clarity.

Watch-out 3: picking people's brains – this phrase isn't helpful when asking for advice. Though well intentioned, it isn't specific or thoughtful enough as a way to ask for advice.

Giving Feedback

The thought of giving feedback can trigger our fear of friction. We may worry about not being able to share feedback in a way that will be useful for someone. But if we keep valuable insights about people's impact to ourselves, we limit our own and other people's learning.

Giving feedback is good for everyone's growth. You have the chance to support someone to do more of what makes them stand out and to close gaps that might be getting in their way. When someone improves their performance, it doesn't only benefit them. It benefits the team they're in and all the people they work with too. Giving feedback increases the likelihood of everyone performing better at work.

Giving Feedback Red Flags

Giving feedback is probably the most difficult of the three feedback skills. Because people find it hard to do, they don't practise it frequently. This can result in red flags that affect the quality of feedback that is shared. Knowing your red flags can help you to see where your approach to giving feedback could be improved.

UNCLEAR IS UNKIND

Your need to be nice can get in the way of someone else's growth. Using waffly words and general statements clouds the clarity of your communication. You won't help someone to get better, whether you want to give feedback about their strengths or share a more difficult message with them.

UNCLEAR FEEDBACK SOUNDS LIKE

> 'Great presentation in the team meeting today, I thought you did a really fantastic job, well done.'

MESSAGE OVERLOAD

Sharing too many messages at once leads to overload for the other person. It might feel efficient to store up lots of feedback to deliver at the same time, but most of what you share will get forgotten. Saying too much at the same time also results in a one-sided conversation, where the other person has less opportunity to get involved in the discussion.

Feedback That Puts Learning First

MESSAGE OVERLOAD SOUNDS LIKE

> 'In your presentations you could try starting with the key messages you'd like to communicate and add in a few more stories. It would also be useful to consider pausing more to let messages sink in and maybe stopping at times to let people ask questions. And it's helpful to ask someone else to review your presentations for easily missed typos. I also love how the insight team are using graphics in their presentations, so maybe there's something you could learn from their approach.'

FEEDBACK SANDWICH

We create confusion by sharing mixed messages. One example of this is the 'feedback sandwich' technique; the idea of sharing a difficult message sandwiched between two positive ones.

FEEDBACK SANDWICH SOUNDS LIKE

> [+] Your organization of the team away day worked really well. I loved the space and the speaker that we had. You also did a brilliant job of bringing lots of energy to the room.
>
> [-] For next time, can you make sure everyone gets the chance to contribute to the day? That's really important and we don't want people to feel excluded or that they've missed out.
>
> [+] But I loved the exercise we did over lunch and I'm already looking forward to our next team day.

There's no research we've found to support the effectiveness of this approach, and hiding hard messages creates multiple challenges:

- **Difficult messages get missed:** this leaves you feeling frustrated and wondering why no change has happened, whereas the other person is unaware any change is needed in the first place.
- **It feels disingenuous:** even if you have the best intentions, delivering feedback in this way can feel misleading. Positive messages aren't believable (even if you meant them) and the person is likely to fixate on the difficult feedback instead.
- **Strengths aren't seen:** the feedback sandwich can mean we waste the opportunity to have a meaningful conversation with someone about what they do well.

Giving Feedback to Accelerate Growth

When we give someone feedback, learning is the goal. Whether we're sharing insights about what someone does well, so they can do it more, or highlighting a potential challenge, our purpose stays the same. We'll now explore two specific techniques for giving feedback:

- **Brilliant Because** – which increases people's awareness of their strengths
- **Say the Hard Thing** – a structure for difficult conversations

Feedback That Puts Learning First

Giving Feedback: *Brilliant Because*

Sharing specific feedback with someone about what they do well leaves them in no doubt about what stood out. Rather than saying 'well done', describing the 'why behind the well done' helps positive messages to sink in. This means people are less likely to dismiss or skip past good news, and more likely to appreciate the value that they add.

BRILLIANT BECAUSE SOUNDS LIKE

- 'I was really impressed with how you handled that situation. It was brilliant because you stayed calm and curious by asking questions to understand the other team's perspective.'

- 'Amazing job hitting that deadline. I know how hard it was to do. You've done a brilliant job of prioritizing your work and asking for the help you needed to make sure you could deliver on this critical piece of work.'

- 'I thought you did a great job in that meeting. Your preparation made all the difference, as we had the required data ready for the important decisions we had to make in the moment.'

Sharing strengths feedback supports people to spot areas they're good at but might have missed or taken for granted. We don't need lengthy conversations or long emails to give *brilliant because* feedback. It can be quick to deliver. Maybe it's a conversation you have with a colleague between meetings or an instant message you send when you have a spare five minutes. When you start to give *brilliant because* feedback, you might be surprised by how this small action can make a significant difference to someone's development.

EXPERT INSIGHT: HOW WE RESPOND TO PRAISE

Receiving praise can prompt us to make jokes, deflect, change the subject, pass the credit or even share what we've not done well to even things out. In a study of more than 400 people, 70 per cent shared that they feel embarrassed and uncomfortable with praise.[19] Christopher Littlefield, an expert in employee appreciation, shares there are three ways we can transform our relationship with praise.

1. Know it's about the giver: accept someone's perspective (even if you don't recognize it) and start by saying a simple 'thank you'.

2. Reframe vulnerability as openness: often the surprise that comes with being praised means we shut down. Instead, see praise as an opportunity to connect with someone, and know that it's okay to acknowledge and say out loud, 'I didn't realize that was a strength I had.'

3. Recognize your learned behaviours: our knee-jerk reactions to praise are often learned from the unspoken rules of recognition in our home growing up. By being curious about why we respond in the way that we do, we can also choose to behave differently, i.e. rather than making a joke or being dismissive, ask a curious question.

Giving Feedback: *Say The Hard Thing*

There will be times when you need to share a difficult message with someone you work with. Maybe your manager has repeatedly cancelled your 121s, and it's left you feeling unsupported. Or perhaps a colleague keeps missing project deadlines, and it's holding the team's progress back. No one gets it right all the time, which means sometimes we need to help people learn what's not working so they can make a choice about what to change.

If we're not confident in delivering a difficult message, we can be too direct in the delivery, which will feel confrontational for the other person. Or if we're worried about how someone might respond, we might be too general and fail to communicate the main message we are trying to deliver. This is when having a conversation structure is useful. We can't control how someone responds to a conversation, but we can be confident about giving feedback in a way that puts learning first.

The 'say the hard thing' conversation structure is not a rigid formula to follow. Every conversation is different because every situation and person is different. Some people will want to talk things through for longer, whereas other people are more direct and want to get straight to the point. However, using this structure will give you enough guidance for a conversation while also allowing space to listen and respond to the other person.

'SAY THE HARD THING' CONVERSATION STRUCTURE
- **Open:** start difficult conversations with a question to better understand someone's situation.
- **Acknowledge:** listen attentively and use what you've heard as part of the conversation.
- **Say the hard thing:** communicate a difficult message in a short and simple way.
- **Involve:** include the other person and hear their perspective.

Learn Like a Lobster

OPEN > ACKNOWLEDGE > SAY THE HARD THING > INVOLVE

How we start sets the tone for a conversation. If we dive straight into what we want to say, it's more likely to result in a defensive response from the other person. Opening a conversation with a question that demonstrates curiosity shifts the focus to the other person and gives them back some control in how they choose to respond.

EXAMPLES OF OPENERS
- 'I'm interested to know how the meetings for Project A are going?'
- 'How are you feeling about progress on the priorities for this quarter?'
- 'We've not caught up for a while, how's the last month been for you?'

OPEN > **ACKNOWLEDGE** > SAY THE HARD THING > INVOLVE

After listening to someone's perspective on a situation, it's important to acknowledge how they're feeling rather than skipping straight to what you want to say. You can do this by repeating words or phrases that you've heard.

EXAMPLES OF ACKNOWLEDGERS
- 'That sounds really frustrating, especially as you've shared that it's happened on more than one occasion.'
- 'This is a tricky situation and you've mentioned a few times how overwhelming it's feeling, which is very understandable.'

- 'That is hard, and I agree it's tough to lead a meeting when lots of strong opinions are being shared by senior people.'

One watch-out when acknowledging how someone feels is unintentionally shifting the conversation to be about you, for example: 'I know exactly how you feel, I've been in this situation and found it hard.' When we shift a conversation away from the person we're talking to, we prioritize our own experiences over the person we are focused on supporting.

> **EXPERT INSIGHT: DON'T BE A CONVERSATIONAL NARCISSIST**
>
> Journalist and writer Celeste Headlee highlights that how we choose to respond in a conversation is an indicator, consciously or unconsciously, of our need for control. A shift response switches the focus of a conversation back to us; a support response keeps the focus of the conversation with the other person.
>
> Example: 'I'm finding work so overwhelming at the moment.'
>
> Shift response: 'Me too! I'm juggling so much, and fitting everything in is such a challenge.'
>
> Support response: 'That's hard. What's causing the overwhelm do you think?'
>
> Headlee shares that though we all shift focus in conversations some of the time, if we're constantly turning the attention back to ourselves, we become a conversational narcissist and it's a signal to other people that we don't care about what they have to say.

'A support response lets someone know you're listening and interested in hearing more.' CELESTE HEADLEE

🔊 Learn more by listening to Celeste Headlee in conversation with Sarah on episode 207 of the *Squiggly Careers* podcast.

OPEN > ACKNOWLEDGE > **SAY THE HARD THING** > INVOLVE

There will be a point in the conversation where you need to take a breath and share the hard message. You know it will feel uncomfortable to say and will be hard to hear, and it's difficult to anticipate how someone is going to react. This is when having a starting statement can be helpful.

EXAMPLES OF 'SAY THE HARD THING' STARTING STATEMENTS
- 'I've noticed that . . .'
- 'From my perspective . . .'
- 'One area I'd like to talk to you about today is . . .'
- 'I have a different point of view. I observe . . .'
- 'When we're in this situation I find that . . .'

EXPERT INSIGHT: EMOTIONAL CONTAGION

'Emotion is part of the equation.'
LIZ FOSSLIEN AND MOLLIE WEST DUFFY

In their brilliantly visual book, *No Hard Feelings*, Liz Fosslien and Mollie West Duffy describe how we usually address feelings at work 'as enemies that need to be wrangled into submission'. They point out that we bring our feelings to work every day, so rather than ignoring them it's better to see our feelings as guideposts. They can be learned from and, when expressed effectively, helpful. It's also important to understand the impact our emotions can have on other people. Fosslien and West Duffy describe a process called 'emotional contagion', where we catch each other's feelings. As humans we're prone to synch our emotions with the people around us, either unconsciously or consciously. If you approach a difficult conversation with anxiety and stress, that's what you're most likely to get in return. Equally, if you're smiling while saying a difficult message, it's confusing for the person listening. However, if you can approach difficult feedback feeling calm, you increase the chances of having a useful conversation.

🔊 Learn more by listening to Mollie West Duffy talking about emotions at work with Sarah on episode 97 of the *Squiggly Careers* podcast.

OPEN > ACKNOWLEDGE > SAY THE HARD THING > **INVOLVE**

After you've said the hard thing, your aim is to involve the other person in the conversation as soon as possible. This could mean involving them in a decision about whether the conversation continues or is paused for the person to process what they've heard and come back together another day. Involving people gives them back control and reduces the risk of a conversation feeling confrontational. Involving doesn't mean solving everything there and then. Learning is much more likely to happen when people are reflecting, questioning and discussing the details with you.

EXAMPLES OF INVOLVERS

- 'What would be useful for you right now? Would you like some time to think before we continue our conversation, or shall we explore more together now?'
- 'What are your first thoughts?'
- 'What would you like to be different by the time we next catch up?'
- 'What's feeling hard for you?'

CASE STUDY: SAY THE HARD THING

Hard feedback you want to give

A team member is dominating meetings by talking too much and interrupting

---

Opener

'I know this is your first time leading a project of this size. How are you finding the meetings so far?'

How do they respond?

Stuck	Defensive	Blind spot
'They're terrible! With so many people involved I find it difficult to keep everyone focused and always get worried we're not going to cover what needs to get done.'	'They're not great. We have too many opinions and not enough action, and I spend lots of time getting people to focus on what matters.'	'They seem to be going well. I'm enjoying working with the team and the chance to work on a project of this size for the first time.'

Feedback That Puts Learning First

What have I learned?

Stuck	Defensive	Blind spot
That the meetings are a source of stress for this person, and they need support.	That the meetings are a source of frustration for this person.	That I have a different perspective to my team member on how well these meetings are going.

What do I say next?

Acknowledge

'That sounds very difficult to navigate.'

Say the hard thing

'I've noticed that you interrupt people, which might be because you want to keep people focused but it also means people get frustrated that they're not contributing.'

Involve the other person

'What would make those meetings work better for you?'

Acknowledge

'It sounds frustrating, having to work hard to keep those meetings on track.'

Say the hard thing

'From my perspective, I've noticed you talk a lot in those sessions and interrupt people, and I wonder if that's because of how you're feeling?'

Involve the other person

'In an ideal world, what would you change about your role in those meetings?'

Acknowledge

'It's good to hear that you're enjoying the experience of working on a bigger project.'

Say the hard thing

'One thing I've spotted that could impact your effectiveness is that you're interrupting frequently in those meetings, which could stop people from sharing their ideas.'

Involve the other person

'From your perspective, is this something you've noticed?'

Receiving Feedback

> 'The ego is like a shield that protects us from feedback, but it also keeps us stuck in old patterns and prevents us from reaching our full potential. To break through that shield, we must be willing to listen, learn and grow.' CAROL DWECK

The feedback we receive from others is a rich source of learning, but only if we listen to what someone has to say. Our ability to be open and process feedback is influenced by how much control we have in a conversation. If we've asked for feedback, we know it's coming, and we're primed and prepared for a response. When we receive feedback unexpectedly, it catches us off guard, and we feel like we have no control. And if it's not a message we're expecting to hear, our instinct can be to get defensive, defeatist or dismissive.

- **Defensive response:** *it's not my fault.*
- **Defeatist response:** *there's nothing I can do about that.*
- **Dismissive response:** *I was just doing my job.*

It's hard to change an instinctive reaction to something that has made us angry, upset, embarrassed or disappointed (or maybe all these emotions at once). This is why it's important to remove the pressure of needing to respond to feedback we receive in the moment.

Think/Feel/Do

Pausing when you receive feedback to consider *what has this made me think, feel and do?* will help you to quickly reflect and move forward.

THINK
- Have I had this feedback before, or is it new to me?
- What do I think about this feedback?
- Who else could I ask for feedback about this area?

FEEL
- How did I feel receiving the feedback in the moment?
- How do I feel a couple of days after receiving the feedback?
- How would I feel about exploring the feedback further with the person who shared it?

DO
- How useful is this feedback on a scale of 1 to 10?
- What have other people done that could work well for me?
- What action (if any) do I want to take now?

EXPERT INSIGHT: NAME IT, TO TAME IT

Feedback, particularly harder-to-hear feedback, can start a roller coaster of emotions. Psychologist Dr Dan Siegel describes how avoiding or supressing our emotions doesn't help us to move forward. The sooner we start noticing and naming how we're feeling, the quicker we can start learning. Siegel calls this process 'name it, to tame it'. We can reduce the impact of our emotions by simply writing them down. We don't need to rationalize or explain why we're feeling this way, naming is enough.

For example, if you've just received the feedback that you were unsuccessful in getting a role you applied for, the emotions you might name could include *disheartened* because you put a lot of effort in, *confused* because you're not sure what to do next, and *disappointed* that you won't get to work in a role you were excited about.

'In the brain, naming an emotion can help calm it.'
DR DAN SIEGEL

🔊 Learn more by listening to the *Squiggly Careers* podcast: *How to Cage Your Confidence Gremlins*.

The Multiplier Effect

To get the highest learning rewards from the feedback we receive, we need to keep revisiting what we heard with as many people as possible. If we don't do this, we're more likely to forget the feedback than to learn from it. Each time we talk to someone about the feedback we've received, it consolidates what we've heard and learned. This is because recollection strengthens the neural networks in our brains that help us to remember information easily and accurately. By sharing the feedback we receive with others, we not only make sure our learning sticks, but we also benefit from other people spotting even more opportunities for us to grow.

There is no limit to who you can share feedback with. Team members can give you support, particularly with difficult feedback. Managers can be helpful in creating the space to put feedback insights into action. Sharing feedback with stakeholders can help them to see the commitment you have to your development, and talking about your feedback with people outside of your business can unlock new ideas and opportunities. Going back to the person who shared the initial feedback with you is also a great way to close the learning loop. It helps the person see that you have taken their feedback on board and that it has made a difference to your development. This means they are more likely to support you in the future and see you as someone who is open to learning and willing to put effort into their growth.

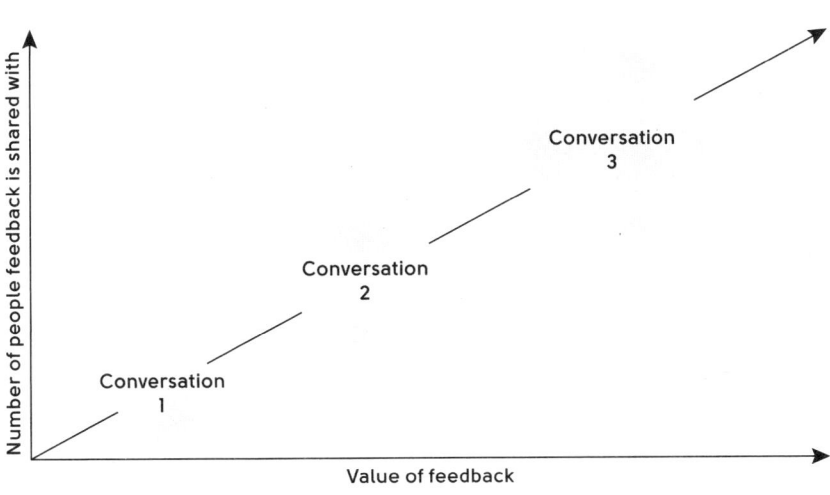

CASE STUDY 1:
THE MULTIPLIER EFFECT IN ACTION

Feedback received from an internal stakeholder:	
'You are often late and rushed in project meetings, and it makes me feel like you are not committed to the project or respectful of other people's time.'	
+ Conversation 1 with your manager:	**++ Conversation 2** with a project team member:
'I received some difficult feedback from my project sponsor who has noticed that I'm often late to meetings and as a result they've questioned my commitment. Though it felt hard to hear, it's made me reflect on the fact that I think I've said yes to too many different pieces of work. I was wondering if we could go through my priorities together today to help resolve this challenge?'	'Our project sponsor shared with me that being late for meetings has impacted my effectiveness. Though I was upset at the time, I've since reflected, and I think they're right. I know you've been working for a while on projects that are always demanding and pull you in different directions. How do you manage to fit things in?'
+++ Conversation 3 with a mentor:	**++++ Conversation 4** with the internal stakeholder:
'I feel like I've really let someone down whose opinion I care about. It's made me nervous about future meetings and conversations with them. What advice would you give me to start rebuilding the trust I'm worried I've lost?'	'Thank you for the feedback. I've taken it seriously and have worked with my manager to reprioritize my workload. I'd like to check in with you regularly, to make sure I'm performing on the project and supporting the team.'

CASE STUDY 2:
THE MULTIPLIER EFFECT IN ACTION

Feedback received from a mentor:	
'You're such a good presenter! It's not something I see you do very often, but your enthusiasm and knowledge really shine through, you're a natural. I wonder if you could present more often, as I think it's a real strength of yours, but it feels a bit hidden at the moment.'	
+ Conversation 1 with a team member:	++ Conversation 2 with your manager:
'I had a really useful chat with my mentor last week and it made me realize how much I enjoy presenting. I know it's something I could get better at if I was doing it more often. What do you think about buddying up and presenting our ideas for the team away day in next week's meeting?'	'My mentor gave me some feedback about how strong they feel my presenting skills are, which isn't really something I've given much thought to. I was wondering whether we could explore more opportunities for me to present, as I've realized it's something I really enjoy and would like to do more of.'
+++ Conversation 3 with a friend:	++++ Conversation 4 with the mentor:
'I've got such a brilliant mentor at the moment. They've really increased my self-belief in my presenting skills, and it's something I'm going to start doing more of. It's really increased my energy at work.'	'Our last conversation together, when you mentioned that my presentation skills stood out to you, has had a really positive impact on me. Since then, I've been presenting more at work. I feel confident and I'm getting involved in lots of new things. I wouldn't have done that without your feedback – thank you!'

What Will I Learn?

To take the initiative and ask, give and receive feedback in a way that puts learning first.

Feedback relies on your initiative to take action and put learning first. No one is going to force you to make feedback a priority. This is one of the reasons that feedback can be challenging; it's a choice to start doing something that you don't do today. Even the easiest actions we've described in this chapter will feel unfamiliar and uncomfortable at first. Once you start using techniques like *framers*, *brilliant because* and the *multiplier effect*, you will feel the difference they make to your development. People will give you insights you haven't had before and share advice you would have previously missed out on.

Putting into practice a learning-first approach to feedback takes initiative. You don't need approval from other people to be proactive about feedback. Taking the initiative will mean you uncover learning that other people leave behind. People who show initiative stand out. They don't wait or expect to be told what to do, they figure it out for themselves. Taking the initiative to ask for, give and receive feedback in a way that puts learning first isn't always easy, but the growth you get in return is worth the effort.

FEEDBACK THAT PUTS LEARNING FIRST: SUMMARY

1. Our fears surrounding feedback make it easier to choose protecting how we see ourselves over seeking out the opportunity to learn.

2. When feedback puts learning first, we grow in a way that we can't achieve alone. Other people can often see our blind spots and strengths in a way that's hard to notice for ourselves.

3. Framing feedback makes it easier to ask for and quicker to receive. By making asks focused, frequent and in the moment, we increase the flow of learning.

4. Asking for advice rather than feedback can reduce your feedback fears and result in more useful and actionable insights for your learning.

5. Giving feedback means that everyone grows. You give people the chance to appreciate their strengths and understand what might be getting in their way. Watch out for three giving feedback red flags; unclear is unkind, message overload and the feedback sandwich.

6. Lots of people don't feel confident enough to deliver difficult feedback. Using the *say the hard thing* structure (open, acknowledge, say the hard thing, involve) will give you some guidance for the conversation alongside allowing space to listen and respond to the other person.

7. When we share the feedback we receive with other people, it creates a multiplier effect for our learning. We benefit from new ideas, insights and support to turn feedback into action that leads to growth.

8. Asking for, giving and receiving feedback takes initiative. People who learn to take initiative stand out from the crowd and benefit from learning that other people leave behind.

DIVE INTO LEARNING LIKE A LOBSTER

- Begin by: giving someone *brilliant because* feedback on their strengths.
- Then try: asking for *what three words?* feedback on your strengths.

CHAPTER 5

How to Learn When Things Go Wrong

'I really think a champion is defined not by their wins but by how they can recover when they fall.'

Serena Williams

Our weeks at work are rarely smooth sailing. We all make mistakes, fail and experience unexpected challenges along the way. Though tough moments are inevitable at work, it doesn't make them any easier to navigate. Whether it's a small mistake, like a typo in a presentation, or a big issue on a project you're leading, we're so preoccupied by trying to fix things fast that learning at the same time feels very hard to do. When things go wrong, it can feel like our only option is to leave learning until later.

Learning like a lobster means when things go wrong, we see challenges as a chance to grow right there and then. We respond to a mistake or failure in a way that sets us up to learn, and then take action to make learning in a hard moment possible.

Limiting Responses

When something goes wrong, we can respond (without even realizing it) in a way that closes down the possibility of learning. We might redirect our efforts away from learning as we'd prefer not to reflect too deeply, or a mistake might trigger a spiral of self-doubt and catastrophizing. Understanding where your reactions limit learning will support you to reframe your response so you can learn in hard moments.

Avoiding

When something goes wrong, you may want to hide away and pretend it didn't happen. By ignoring or avoiding the issue, you hope it might disappear or go unnoticed. Confronting a mistake feels intimidating and risky, whereas hiding feels safe and reassuring.

Sounds like – *I'm so embarrassed I didn't send that document to our client. If I don't mention it again, hopefully they'll just forget about it. Maybe I can leave my colleague to go on the call with them later, they probably don't need me anyway.*

Overanalysing

When something goes wrong, you become fixated on trying to understand exactly what happened. You spend lots of time reliving a mistake in search of an 'a-ha' moment that will help you make sense of the situation.

Sounds like – *why didn't I send that document to our client? Was it because I was distracted, or maybe in the back of my mind I didn't think it was ready? What else happened that day that meant that I missed it?*

Redirecting

When something goes wrong, you press fast forward and skip onto something else. You avoid reflection, for fear of what you might discover, and move on so you can stay positive and upbeat.

Sounds like – *ah, I forgot to send that document to a client. Never mind, there's no point dwelling on it, that won't help anyone. I'll just get started on the pitch I need to put together instead.*

Pessimism

When something goes wrong, you become your own worst critic. You assume everything is your fault and over apologize for mistakes. You struggle to see any positives, and your pessimism can spill over into the rest of your work and life.

Sounds like – *I can't believe I forgot to send that document to a client, it's such a basic mistake to make. I don't think I'm good enough to do this job, nothing is going well at the moment.*

Learning Reframes

Whether you see yourself in one or all of these responses, what they have in common is that they direct our energy somewhere other than learning.

> *'In any given moment we have two options: to step forward into growth or to step back into safety.'*
> Abraham Maslow

Reframing the way we respond is how we start learning when things go wrong. Hard times are never easy, but by setting ourselves up for learning we can turn a tough time into an accelerator for our growth.

WHEN THINGS GO WRONG

Limiting response	Learning reframe
Avoiding: If I ignore this mistake, hopefully it'll go away, or no one will notice.	Accountability: By sharing mistakes, I get the support that I need.
Zooming In: By analysing the ins/outs of what went wrong, I'll figure out all the answers myself.	Zooming Out: When something goes wrong, I consider different points of view to find the best solution.
Redirecting: When something goes wrong, I shift my focus in a different direction.	Reflecting: I understand what went wrong so I can learn and be better, now and the next time.
Pessimism: When I fail, I'm a failure.	Optimism: Failing is tough, but it won't feel like this forever.

How to Learn When Things Go Wrong

When things go wrong, there's a lot to deal with emotionally and practically. Learning can feel like an extra burden at a time when we're already under pressure. Seeing learning as something separate from a hard moment puts us in an unhelpful frame of mind. We become so focused on moving forward that we don't stop and reflect on what could be done differently. It's a help, not a hindrance, when work is challenging.

How to Learn When Things Go Wrong

Learning is how we make what's gone wrong, right again.

By learning we figure out what needs fixing faster, we see a situation more clearly and can persevere in a way that's much more likely to find a solution. We can't control when things go wrong, but we can make a choice to view a challenge as a chance to learn.

In the rest of this chapter, we focus on actions you can take to learn when things go wrong. These actions are designed to be doable during a hard moment. Of course, they still require some effort from you but in a way that we know is achievable, no matter what else is going on. Over the past ten years, many of the actions we share in this section have been adopted by us and the organizations we work with, so we've seen first-hand the impact they have and the difference they make to people's development.

HOW TO LEARN WHEN THINGS GO WRONG

Learning	Action
Accountability	Mistake moments
Zooming out	Distancers
Reflecting	What worked well? / even better if?
Optimism	Very small successes

Accountability

> 'Professionals should not be afraid to make mistakes. They should be afraid of not learning from the ones they do make.' SIDNEY DEKKER

Avoiding, ignoring or hiding from our mistakes and failures often feels safer than taking accountability for them. Owning our errors may feel vulnerable and exposing in a moment when we're already feeling guilty, threatened and fearful of being judged.

Why We Don't Take Accountability

Blame game
When our ego is in charge, we blame other people if things go wrong. Deflecting accountability feels more comfortable than confronting our own limitations and shortcomings.

Missing role models
If we don't see other people taking accountability for their mistakes, we conclude that it's better to avoid talking about what's gone wrong in favour of highlighting what's going well.

Short-termism
A fast fix might feel like an effective response to a mistake, but it doesn't reflect what it really means to take accountability. When we take full accountability for what went wrong, we go beyond short-term resolutions and think about what we can do

to make sure an issue doesn't happen again for us or the people we work with.

EXPERT INSIGHT: BREAKING THE NAME, BLAME, SHAME CYCLE

Two very different kinds of organization have worked hard to break the 'name, blame, shame' cycle: the NHS, a public sector healthcare organization in the UK, and Etsy, the online marketplace. The cycle of responding to mistakes with a 'point the finger' mindset means that, rather than accepting errors are part and parcel of work, individuals are made to feel like a mistake is their fault. Both the NHS and Etsy have been inspired by the work of professor and part-time pilot Sidney Dekker. Dekker's work focuses on how to create a Just Culture, where the aim is to balance safety and accountability.

One of the simple changes Mersey Care NHS Foundation Trust have made is that when a mistake is made, their response has shifted from *who* is responsible to *what* is responsible. This is part of a larger culture shift to create an environment where people feel safe to speak up and share mistakes, with an emphasis on reflection and learning rather than blaming.

Engineers at Etsy are encouraged to share 'Second Stories' when a mistake is made. The first story about a mistake is often what *should have been done*, which leads to looking for scapegoats, and silence rather than sharing mistakes. The second story is *owned by the engineers*, who identify how a mistake has been made and suggest potential solutions for the future. Engineers, problem solvers by nature, become accountable for, and enthusiastic about, helping the company avoid the same error in the future.[20]

How Taking Accountability Makes Us Smarter

Avoiding our mistakes and failures limits our learning and makes it more likely that we'll repeat the same 'wrongs' in the future. Research has shown that we frequently fail to learn from past errors,[21] because our brains love short cuts, described as 'heuristics', which tell us how to behave in a situation. These short cuts lead to mistake pathways that prompt us to approach a task in the same way and in turn increase the likelihood that we make the same mistakes, again and again. By taking accountability when things go wrong, we increase the likelihood that we learn from rather than repeat errors.

- Avoiding mistakes means we're more likely to repeat them.
- Accountability for mistakes is how we learn for next time.

Small mistakes offer a significant learning opportunity. These are the mistakes that are most likely to get missed and where learning is more likely to be lost. Being more aware of and accountable for the small mistakes you make along the way creates lots of new moments of learning at work.

How to Take Accountability: Mistake Moments

Mistake moments are a way of taking accountability for the small errors we all make at work. This could be forgetting to send an email, responding to someone with the wrong information or missing out an important data point in a presentation. This is why attaching the word 'moment' to a mistake is helpful. It reminds us that mistakes are temporary; we can move past the moment, but by taking accountability the learning comes with us and benefits other people too. Mistake moments increase our accountability and train our brain to look for the learning when things go wrong.

EXAMPLES OF MISTAKE MOMENTS

EMAIL ERROR

- **Mistake moment:** I copied someone into an email that wasn't intended for them, which didn't look very professional.
- **Learned:** it's a bad idea to reply to work emails in the evening when I'm tired. It seemed efficient at the time, but it ended up creating stress that I could have done without!
- **Action:** I'm going to experiment with blocking in two separate hours during the day to respond to emails, and remove other distractions during that time.

HOLIDAY HANDOVER

- **Mistake moment:** I forgot to hand over some information before going on holiday, which has delayed a project from moving forward.
- **Learned:** not to rely on my head to hold all the information I need, especially in a busy period.
- **Action:** before my next holiday, I've scheduled in time two days before I go away to prepare a handover.

MISSED DEADLINE

- **Mistake moment:** yesterday I missed a deadline for responding to a request from a client.

- **Learned:** I've said yes to way too many actions this week. I was trying to be helpful, but in hindsight it was completely unrealistic and left me feeling really overwhelmed.

- **Action:** I want to practise some new ways to say 'not yet' when asked to add more work into my week, and to make my priorities more visible for others.

How to Use Mistake Moments

From using mistake moments in our own organization and the companies we work with, we have discovered a few principles that will support you to maximize how much you learn from the process.

Fast

As soon as a mistake is made (ideally the same day) share the mistake using an online platform like Teams, Slack or WhatsApp.

Short

Limit sharing your mistakes to a few sentences rather than an essay. A simple structure can keep your descriptions short, for example: *Today I had a mistake moment when . . . I learned that . . . next time I will . . .*

Track

If you can keep all your mistake moments in the same place, it makes it easier to spot trends and themes. You might see you're making the same mistake. Or maybe your mistakes seem different on the surface, but you realize they're a result of the same underlying challenge, like being in a rush or not asking for help.

Pilot

If you're doing this for the first time, you could agree with your team to pilot mistake moments for the next three months. A pilot reduces the pressure of trying out a new idea and encourages feedback along the way.

Revisit to reflect

Every few months, take the time to review your mistake moments by yourself or as part of a team. This will help you to spot any recurring trends, and if you're taking this action as a team it creates a sense of shared responsibility.

EXPERT INSIGHT: WHAT HEALTHY FAILURE FEELS LIKE IN A TEAM

> 'Psychological safety in a team is virtually synonymous with a learning environment in a team.'
> **AMY EDMONDSON**

In a psychologically safe team, it's safe to speak up, ask for help and constructively challenge. In her book *Right Kind of Wrong*, Edmondson defines 'intelligent failure' as work that involves novelty, uncertainty and interdependence. In these situations, the risk of failing is worth the potential reward of succeeding and, if done right, the guarantee of learning. When working with teams, she encourages them to evaluate what percentage of time they spend in a week on the left-hand side of the table below versus the right-hand side.

HOW MUCH OF WHAT YOU CURRENTLY HEAR IS . . .

This		This
Good news		Bad news
Progress	Versus	Problems
Agreement		Dissent
All's well		I need help

Edmondson makes the point that what *feels good* in a team is probably *not* good from the perspective of a healthy failure culture, where people can speak up with problems, concerns and questions. Where teams have a healthy failure culture, people have a shared belief that learning and failing go hand in hand, and that makes it easier to speak up quickly.

🔊 Learn more by listening to Amy Edmondson on episodes 151 and 373 of the *Squiggly Careers* podcast.

Zooming Out

When we want to understand what went wrong, it's easy to dive straight into the details. We attempt to analyse exactly what happened as well as how it happened. We keep digging for more and more data and information, in the hope this will provide us with answers. We end up zooming in so much that we lose sight of what's most important. Zooming out when things go wrong helps us to see a situation from a distance, and this gives us different insights for our learning.

How to Zoom Out: Distancers

'Perspective is necessary. Otherwise, you live with your face squashed up against a wall, everything a huge foreground.'

Margaret Atwood

To zoom out we need to get some distance from our situation. Distance is particularly useful when there's complexity and emotion surrounding what's gone wrong. It's also helpful when you're closely involved in an issue and want to make sure you can see the situation from other people's perspective. Zooming out is quick to do once you have a few techniques that work for you. We've created four different distancers that will support you to zoom out fast, as they all take less than fifteen minutes to do. Each distancer is something you can action yourself, because though talking to other people is also a helpful technique, that option might not always be available to you in the moment when you need some perspective.

- **Third-person viewpoint:** imagining an outside-in view of what's gone wrong.
- **Fly-on-the-wall facts:** gaining distance from your and others' feelings to focus on the facts.
- **Swap shoes:** seeing your situation through other people's perspective.
- **Time travel:** rewinding and fast-forwarding to gain perspective on the present.

DISTANCER 1: THIRD-PERSON VIEWPOINT

> '**You see, but you do not observe. The distinction is clear.**' SHERLOCK HOLMES TO WATSON

Seeing our situation with a third-person perspective disconnects us, briefly, from the thoughts, feelings and actions that could be clouding our judgement when things go wrong. Applying third-person thinking to yourself can feel a bit strange, but the indirect nature of asking questions in this way gives us an outside-in view of our situation. This can support us to get unstuck and identify actions so we can make progress.

EXAMPLES OF THIRD-PERSON QUESTIONS
- Who could help Sarah?
- What questions does Sarah need to ask?
- What action is Sarah avoiding that would be useful?
- What is Sarah missing about this situation?
- What does Sarah do well when things go wrong?
- How are Sarah's feelings helping or hindering her?
- What is stopping Sarah taking an action that's important?

EXPERT INSIGHT: THE POWER OF SELF-DISTANCING

'By taking a step back and observing ourselves as if we were another person, we can significantly reduce the emotional charge of the situation, which in turn allows us to think more clearly and make better decisions.'
ETHAN KROSS

Psychologist Ethan Kross found that participants who adopted a self-distanced perspective when reflecting on negative experiences reported lower levels of emotional distress compared to those who reflected on their experiences from a self-immersed perspective. This difference can be as simple as saying to ourselves: *Sarah is having a tough day, as she had a difficult project meeting* versus *I'm having a tough day, that project meeting was a disaster.*

His work has also shown that when people have tools to create psychological distance, they are able to consider the bigger picture, make less impulsive decisions and get better at solving problems.

🔊 Learn more by listening to Sarah explore self-belief with Ethan Kross on episode 254 of the *Squiggly Careers* podcast.

DISTANCER 2: FLY-ON-THE-WALL FACTS

When we see our situation as if we were a fly on the wall, we observe events with a neutral and objective eye. A fly can only see what's happening, they're not involved, so their focus is on the facts. This gives us a stripped-back version of events, which can be helpful if you feel overwhelmed by your or other people's emotions when something goes wrong.

FLY-ON-THE-WALL FACTS
- Imagine you're a fly buzzing above and around what's gone wrong. You're observing and listening but not involved in what's happening.
- You can only see what a fly would see: actions and behaviours. You don't know what people are thinking or feeling.

- Write down the facts of the situation. A useful prompt is: *What do I know to be 100 per cent true about this situation?*

EXPERT INSIGHT: ARE YOU A VICTIM OR A VILLAIN?

In her book *Reality-based Leadership* Cy Wakeman points out that our stress is often not caused by the facts of a situation but by the stories we tell ourselves about what happens to us. Wakeman highlights three story watch-outs to be wary of:

1. Victim stories: *it's not my fault*
2. Villain stories: *it's all your fault*
3. Helpless stories: *there's nothing I can do*

Wakeman suggests that most of us don't realize how 'deeply attached we are to being right and to the approval of others'. To be able to accurately see the reality of a situation requires us to give our ego a rest and let go of being defensive. In particular, she points out that when things go wrong, we need to swap justifying, blaming and being stubborn for a drive towards results and learning. This drive to learn prevents us from being a victim of our circumstances and removes what she describes as 'the emotional drain and drama' that can happen when things go wrong.

DISTANCER 3: SWAP SHOES

When something goes wrong, it's easy to assume everyone cares about the same things as you, but people have their own priorities, goals and objectives, which inform how they see a situation.

By putting yourself in other people's shoes, you can gain insights that might impact or change how you approach fixing a failure or navigating something that has gone wrong.

SWAP SHOES WITH

- **Your manager:** How does what's gone wrong impact your manager? What are they most likely to be concerned about? What are they likely to be thinking about?

- **Your team:** What impact is this mistake going to have on your team? What questions and concerns will it raise for them? What support are they likely to need to be able to move forward?

- **Your stakeholders:** What do the teams connected to this challenge care about? For example, if it's a marketing or sales team, maybe it's the impact on customers. If it's a finance team, how will a process failing impact revenue or cash flow?

DISTANCER 4: TIME TRAVEL

When something goes wrong, our focus on what's happening right now can mean we forget to learn from what's gone before and don't look ahead to where we're going. Some quick rewinding and fast-forwarding will give you a new perspective on what you're experiencing.

Your experiences of when things have gone wrong before are useful examples to learn from. You will remind yourself of techniques and actions that have worked in the past that could be useful today.

REWIND TIME TRAVEL QUESTIONS
- When I last made a mistake, what helped me move forward?
- What do I regret not doing when something went wrong at work previously?
- What have I seen other people do well when they've made a mistake?
- What advice have I given people before, when they've had a hard time at work?
- When I've failed before, who supported me?

Looking ahead can give you a purpose beyond the problem. It won't make a mistake disappear, but it will give you a boost of motivation to work through it.

FAST-FORWARD TIME TRAVEL QUESTIONS
- What do I want people to say about me and this mistake six months from now?
- What will I care about when I look back at this moment?
- What do I want to be true in one month's time that isn't true today?
- If I imagine I'm five years older, how do I think the future me would describe this situation?
- What can I practise doing now so that it's easier for me in the future?

EXPERT INSIGHT:
HOW TO MAKE THE UNIMAGINABLE, IMAGINABLE

> 'Episodic future thinking or EFT is often described as "mental time travel" – your brain is working to help you see and feel the future as clearly and vividly as if you were already there.' JANE MCGONIGAL

Futurist and game designer Jane McGonigal advocates futures thinking as a practical tool to 'prepare your mind to adapt faster to new challenges, build hope and resilience, reduce anxiety and depression, and inspire you to take actions today that set yourself up for future happiness and success'.[22]

McGonigal shares how imagining the future forces your brain to draw on past experiences and invent new possibilities. Imagining is playing with, rather than escaping, reality. It's a way of discovering risks and opportunities that weren't immediately obvious.

You can apply future thinking to your career by imagining different time horizons – for example, looking ahead by six months, two years and ten years – and imagining what you want your work and time at work to look like. Useful prompts might be: *What are you working on? Who are you working with? How are you working?* The further into the future you go, the harder your brain has to work to fill in the blank spaces. McGonigal believes this supports us to practise imagining the unimaginable and, rather than dismissing our future as a pipe dream, prompts us to start considering the actions we might want to take today to prepare us for the future. McGonigal views imagination training as a powerful decision-making and motivational tool. It supports us to spot what we need to change to make a future more or less likely.

Reflecting

When something goes wrong, reflection in the moment rarely feels like a priority. However, leaving reflection until later means we lose lots of in-the-moment learning. The details of what happened and how different people played a part become harder to remember as time passes. This is why meetings such as 'post-implementation reviews' don't always feel useful, as recency bias (our tendency to focus on recent events and forget what's gone before) gets in the way of being specific and accurate about what we've learned.

It's not just the rush to resolve an issue that can make reflecting in the moment hard. Our preference towards thinking or doing can also impact the way that we reflect. If you're a natural doer, your rush to resolve a problem can mean you miss the chance to learn. If you're a thinker, you can be lost in rumination and stop things from moving forward. Successful in-the-moment reflection is a balance of thinking and doing. Bringing the two together is how we get the best results from time spent reflecting.

HOW A DOER PREFERENCE CAN GET IN THE WAY OF REFLECTION

- **In a rush:** doers focus on speed over slowing down and they can feel frustrated by pressing pause on progress to make space to reflect.
- **On repeat:** doers have a need to 'get it done', which can mean they default to what they've done before rather than considering alternative options.
- **On their own:** doers can be so driven to make things happen that they forget to involve other people in the process.

How to Learn When Things Go Wrong

HOW A THINKER PREFERENCE CAN GET IN THE WAY OF REFLECTION

- **Rumination:** thinkers think deeply and thoughtfully, but this can lead to rumination rather than getting to useful insight and actions.
- **Analysis paralysis:** thinkers consider all the different angles and possibilities but, overloaded with information, they can experience analysis paralysis.
- **Opinion overload:** thinkers are interested in other people's perspective, but conflicting opinions can create confusion and make it hard to move forward.

How to Balance Thinking and Doing for Reflection

Being more aware of your thinker/doer preference helps you to spot where you might be getting in the way of your own learning. When we combine the best things about being a thinker and a doer, we can reflect in a way that combines awareness and action, and learn more in return.

BENEFITS OF THINKING AND DOING FOR REFLECTION

- Noticing the need to pause for thought, without procrastinating
- Reflecting in a way that doesn't rely on waiting for a meeting
- Using a simple process that's easy to remember and quick to do

EXPERT INSIGHT: DOING BY LEARNING

> 'Learning-by-doing doesn't separate thinking from doing, in fact it brings the two together.' DAVID ERIXON[23]

David Erixon, co-founder of Hyper Island and business leader, proposes that learning-by-doing would be better explained using the phrase 'learning through reflection on doing' or perhaps even better 'doing by learning'. Erixon points out that learning is too often seen as something that happens *after* the work has been completed. Instead, he argues that reflective thinking needs to be part of the process.

🔊 Learn more by listening to David Erixon in conversation with Sarah on episode 317 of the *Squiggly Careers* podcast.

How to Reflect in Real Time

Reflection is how we transform experience into meaning and make sense of what's happening. If we don't reflect when we make a mistake, fail or experience unexpected challenges, we risk reverting back to unhelpful responses like avoiding or redirecting (explored at the start of Part 2).

What Worked Well? / Even Better If?

For reflection to work when things go wrong it needs to be quick, easy and memorable.

Here is one simple technique for immediate reflection:

- What worked well? (WWW)
- What would be even better if – for next time? (EBI)

This reflection technique has lots of advantages:

Noticing

WWW/EBI is a practical way to create a continual improvement mindset. The more we use the technique, the easier it becomes to notice learning that might have passed us by previously.

Balanced

Reflecting on both WWW and EBI stops our negativity bias going into overdrive. In a moment when we're typically giving ourselves a hard time, it forces us to acknowledge what we've done well.

Flexible

WWW/EBI is a tool that you can use by yourself or as a group. It works equally well whether your team are all together in the office, work in a hybrid way or remotely.

Action

Using WWW/EBI stops us getting distracted by what we wish we'd done but now can't change. Looking ahead to what we want to make even better next time creates clear actions that we feel in control of.

EXPERT INSIGHT:
WHY THE SMARTEST PEOPLE MAKE THE WORST LEARNERS

In his book *Teaching Smart People How to Learn*, the late Harvard professor Chris Argyris observed an interesting dilemma: successful people rarely fail, and as a result when they do, they don't know how to learn from the experience. Argyris noticed that these individuals were much more likely to feel threatened, defensive and to project blame elsewhere when they experienced failure. Argyris states that the challenge is how to teach people to examine their behaviour in a new way that breaks down the barriers that block learning. These barriers are, he argues, based on a universal tendency to design our actions according to four motivations:

1. to stay in control
2. to maximize winning and minimize losing
3. to suppress negative feelings
4. to be as 'rational' as possible

The purpose of these motivations is to avoid embarrassment or feeling threatened, vulnerable or incompetent. The challenge for the organizations studied by Argyris was how to support people to let go of defensive reasoning in favour of open inquiry.

One technique Argyris used was real-life case studies that gave managers the chance to practise reflecting on their own behaviours, to promote continual improvement. He noticed that conversations started changing from complaining about others to constructive understanding and accountability. By the end of the process he observed: 'They are laying the groundwork for continuous improvement that is truly continuous. They are learning how to learn.'

How to Use WWW/EBI

There are lots of different ways you can use WWW/EBI to reflect when things go wrong. To bring this to life we're going to explore three different hard moment scenarios and show how reflection using this technique can be helpful for learning.

HARD MOMENT SCENARIOS

1. **Surprise hard moment:** an unexpected mistake or failure
2. **We're in it together hard moment:** shared experience of something going wrong
3. **Long-haul hard moment:** a tough time that is here to stay

Surprise Hard Moment

It's Tuesday and you're expecting it to be a normal day at work. Then something goes wrong that takes you by surprise. The issue came out of nowhere, and you're now wondering how a day that started so well could have so quickly taken a turn for the worse.

WWW/EBI MULTIPLIED BY THE POWER OF THREE

Our brains respond well to things that come in threes.[24] Three seems to be just enough information for our brains to process before we get bored or distracted. Straight after a moment when something has gone wrong, try completing a WWW/EBI × 3 table, like the examples below. Reflecting in threes makes this exercise long enough to be useful but short enough to be something you can do quickly. Using three of each will also prompt you to search for the *what worked well* insights – which are there, but less immediately obvious – and limit the *even better ifs* – which are front of mind, so we're tempted to continue listing them.

WWW/EBI × 3

The technology failed in my presentation	
WWW?	EBI?
1. I stayed calm on stage when the technology failed.	1. Have a tech practice session for important presentations.
2. I knew my work well enough to share key points without slides.	2. Build in contingency so I have time to fix tech issues.
3. I answered a challenging question with confidence.	3. If tech doesn't work, know my back-up plan.

WWW/EBI × 3

My manager is disappointed that I didn't let them know about a missed deadline	
WWW?	EBI?
1. I had already taken action to reduce the impact of the delay.	1. I produced a status report, so I didn't need to remember everything.
2. The project team were aware and supportive of the new plan.	2. I held a monthly senior stakeholder meeting to answer questions.
3. I wasn't defensive when challenged by my manager.	3. I had a better understanding of my manager's needs from the project.

We're in it Together Hard Moment

You're working as part of a cross-functional project team, and you've run into a serious roadblock. An important process that impacts your customers has failed. As a group you're under a lot of pressure to figure out a solution fast. Working out what went wrong and what to do now is going to be a joint effort, and likely to involve some challenging conversations.

WWW/EBI MULTIPLIED BY BRAIN WRITING

It's easy to imagine how exploring *what worked well* and *even better if* as a group could end up being unwieldy and unstructured. Senior people can end up dominating discussions, and those closest to the learning don't get the chance or have the confidence to share. This is where brain writing can be a useful technique to try. Brain writing is typically used as an ideation technique where people write down their ideas in silence before sharing them. It's designed to feel safe, inclusive and to encourage more introverted personalities and junior team members to participate equally.

If you're experiencing a hard moment as a team, including a WWW/EBI × brain writing reflection increases the opportunity for everyone to learn. You can try this in a few different ways, depending on how your team works. We've included some examples to show what this could look like in practice.

EXAMPLES OF WWW/EBI × BRAIN WRITING

- If you're in a meeting to discuss what's gone wrong, start with two minutes of silence. In that time ask everyone to write down *what worked well* for the project so far and their most significant *even better if*. After two minutes, each person reads out what they've written, with no interruptions or discussions.

- When something goes wrong, ask everyone to share their WWW/EBI that day using an anonymous, free survey tool like Typeform. Anonymity is useful in reducing evaluation apprehension, where we worry that we don't have the right 'answer'.[25] This approach also works well if your team is geographically distributed and works at different times.

- Daily virtual WWW/EBI huddle. If you're working on a fast-moving project with a mixture of small mistakes and big issues, begin each day with team members capturing a WWW from yesterday and what would be an EBI for today. This only needs to take a couple of minutes and can be done using a Teams or Slack channel.

Long-Haul Hard Moment

Your team is being restructured and it's likely to result in job losses. You've been told that the process is going to take a few months, so life at work is going to feel uncertain for a while. The restructure impacts you personally, and it's also likely to affect making progress on some of the projects that you're responsible for. It's going to be an unsettling and hard few months.

WWW/EBI MULTIPLIED BY PEOPLE AND PROGRESS

Academic and psychologist Angela Duckworth describes grit as 'passion and perseverance over time'. This is what we need when we're in a long-haul hard moment where something significant has gone wrong and there's not a quick fix that will make it better. During this time it's helpful to reflect on the role people play in your resilience, and the progress you have already made. Using WWW/EBI to reflect on people and progress helps you to regain perspective when things seem out of your control, and identify actions to stop you feeling stuck.

EXAMPLE 1:
MY TEAM IS BEING RESTRUCTURED AND THE PROCESS WILL TAKE TWO MONTHS

	What's working well?	Even better if?
People	I've spent time with other people internally who are sharing this experience, and it's made me appreciate that I'm not alone.	I spend time with people outside of the organization to give me a new and different perspective on my situation.
Progress	I've updated my CV and LinkedIn profile, and it's given me greater clarity about my achievements.	I set up meetings with people in different parts of my organization to be proactive about exploring other opportunities.

EXAMPLE 2:
MY MANAGER AND I AREN'T WORKING WELL TOGETHER

	What's working well?	Even better if?
People	I've shared my concerns with HR, and I feel like I have been listened to.	I spoke to some people who have been in this position before and got their advice.
Progress	I've started to write down my conversations so I have details to refer back to, and can be clear about my feedback.	I agreed a specific action plan so I am clear about what better looks like and have some goals to work towards.

EXAMPLE 3:
I'M IN A JOB I DON'T ENJOY BUT I'M NOT IN A POSITION TO LEAVE

	What's working well?	Even better if?
People	I have been spending time with a professional network, and that's given me back some energy.	I joined an internal network or employee resource group.
Progress	I've had two curious career conversations in the last month to learn about other people's squiggly careers.	I reconnected with my previous mentor for a meeting in the next few weeks.

EXPERT INSIGHT:
THE COURAGE TO REFLECT ON FAILURE

Researchers James Bailey and Scheherazade Rehman asked 442 executives to identify which experiences most advanced their development and increased their impact as leaders. Leaders shared that reflection on surprise, frustration and failure proved to be most valuable in helping them to grow.[26]

Bailey and Rehman conclude that reflecting when something doesn't go to plan or feels hard takes courage but at the same time will give you motivation to move forward. Reflection in these moments prompts people to be self-aware, explore their potential and feel empowered about the future.

Optimism

> 'Optimism is the faith that leads to achievement. Nothing can be done without hope and confidence.' **HELEN KELLER**

No one plans for things to go wrong, and when they do it's normal to feel more pessimistic than optimistic. The danger with pessimism is that, if left unchecked, it can start to dominate your thinking and determine your actions. When you notice what pessimism sounds like for you, it will act as a signal to add some boosts of optimism into your day.

What Does Your Pessimism Sound Like?

- **It's My Fault:** you're hard on yourself.
- **It's My Life:** everything feels hard all at once.
- **It's My Future:** this is going to be hard forever.

EXAMPLES OF HOW PESSIMISM CAN PERMEATE YOUR THINKING

YOU'RE UNEXPECTEDLY MADE REDUNDANT – WHAT DO YOU THINK?

This feels like my fault	Everything feels hard at the moment	I can't see how life is going to get better
Sounds like: I didn't perform well enough in that role and that's why I've been made redundant. I really only have myself to blame.	Sounds like: Everything is going wrong at the moment. I've been made redundant, I'm not on top of things that need sorting at home, I haven't used my gym membership in months.	Sounds like: This redundancy is going to impact the rest of my career. I can't see how I'm going to get another job as good as this one. This is going to mean I go backwards in my career.

YOU MADE A BIG MISTAKE ON A PROJECT – WHAT DO YOU THINK?

This feels like my fault	Everything feels hard at the moment	I can't see how life is going to get better
Sounds like: I can't believe I didn't spot this and prevent the mistake from happening.	Sounds like: I'm making so many mistakes at the moment, it feels like I can't do anything right.	Sounds like: Everyone is going to remember that I made this mistake, it's going to impact my reputation and stop me being able to progress.

EXPERT INSIGHT:
THE POWER OF BAD

In their book *The Power of Bad* John Tierney and Roy F. Baumeister share what we all instinctively feel, that negative events and emotions affect us more strongly than positive ones. Our negativity bias, an ancient survival response, means we can't help but devote more brain power to processing the things that go wrong rather than the things that go right. Tierney and Baumeister suggest some ways to use what we know about negativity to reduce its power over our thoughts and actions

Stay present
Keep your attention focused on the here and now, rather than dwelling on past negative events or worrying about what could go wrong in the future

Share and celebrate good news
Sharing good news with other people increases its impact and creates connection.

Rule of four ratio
Look for four positive experiences/comments for every negative one. For example, when you've made a mistake, this could look like quickly reminding yourself of four successes you've had so far this year.

Work With Your Worries

> 'Happiness and freedom begin with a clear understanding of one principle: some things are within our control, and some things are not.'
> **EPICTETUS**

When things go wrong, the goal is not to be relentlessly positive. Pretending everything is okay when it's not works *against* and not *for* us. Ignoring our negative thoughts means they're more likely to stay with us for longer. Being overly upbeat also impacts the people around us; if we're observed being too positive in the context of challenges, it looks like we've misjudged the seriousness of a situation.

Before taking an action to build your optimism, it's important that you work with your worries. If your worries are left unchecked when things go wrong, they become unwieldy and are likely to spill over into more pessimism. Simply answering the question 'What am I worried about?' as specifically as possible is a good way to start working with your worries. To move beyond listing your worries, try categorizing them into three areas:

1. worries within my control
2. worries I can influence
3. worries outside my control

A range of research has proved the usefulness of being able to determine what we can and can't control.[27] Making this distinction when things go wrong will increase your resilience, support you to stay calm and mean you're more likely to experience positive emotions.

> **Working with our worries, rather than avoiding them, is how we feel better when things go wrong.**

How to Learn When Things Go Wrong

EXAMPLE: WORK WITH YOUR WORRIES

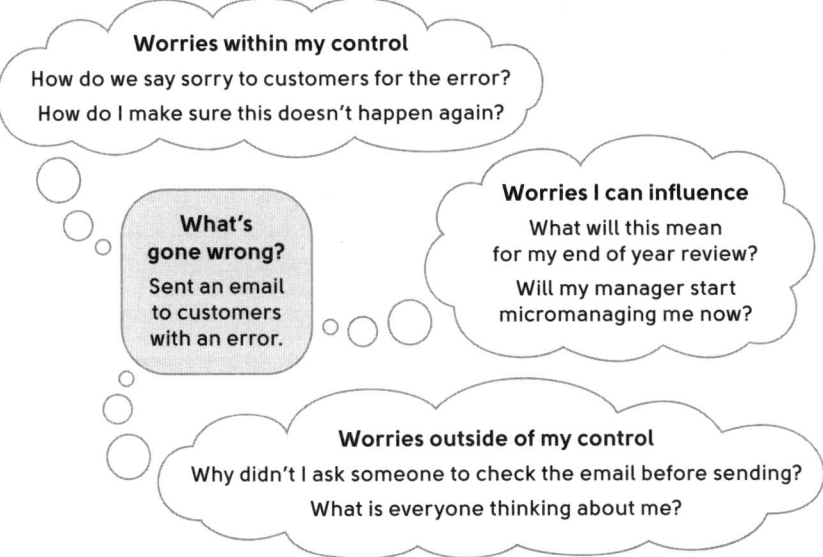

How to Be Optimistic: Very Small Successes

Big wins are easy to see and obvious moments for celebration. However, they're also rare, especially when things go wrong, so relying on them as opportunities to increase our optimism isn't realistic. A more helpful approach is to focus on our very small successes, the ones that happen every day but that we skip past or don't even see.

Recognizing and recording your very small successes is a practical way of adding some optimism into your day. This technique can be particularly helpful in hard moments, when you're surrounded by challenges and success of any sort feels far away.

HOW TO RECORD YOUR VERY SMALL SUCCESSES

- At the end of each day for a week write down 3 very small successes:
    - these can be work successes, home successes or a combination of both.
    - they can include your own successes and supporting other people to succeed.
- Write down your successes in the same place each day.
- At the end of the week, you will have a stack of 21 very small successes.

VERY SMALL SUCCESSES

	Success #1	Success #2	Success #3
Day 1	Went to the gym before work	Helped a colleague with an Excel spreadsheet	Raised a challenge with my manager
Day 2	Made time for a lunch break in a busy day	Asked some good questions in a hard meeting	Got back home for bedtime with my kids
Day 3	Shared a project update	Had coffee with a colleague who has experienced similar challenges to my project	Prepared for my 121 with my manager, which improved the focus of our conversation
Day 4			
Day 5			

How to Learn When Things Go Wrong

Day 6			
Day 7			
Total = 21 successes			

Putting our successes in the same place each day gives us a boost of optimism as our brains respond positively to seeing our successes stacking up. The first few days of spotting and recording your very small successes may feel difficult, and you might need to look back at your diary for inspiration. By day three or four it will start to get easier, and you might even get to the point where your successes are front of mind at the end of a day. Don't be tempted to stop writing them down though, as it's the combination of both recognizing *and* recording our very small successes that gives us the optimism we need.

Noticing and making a note of your very small successes doesn't mean mistakes, failures and disappointments disappear, but it does shine a spotlight on what's going well, even in the middle of a hard moment.

EXPERT INSIGHT:
THE POWER OF SMALL WINS

In their research Teresa Amabile and Steven Kramer, authors of *The Progress Principle*, found that 28 per cent of small events triggered big reactions at work. This is useful, as incremental progress and minor milestones are much more common than achieving long-term goals. For example, a small win like a productive conversation with a manager, or solving a small problem, can have a powerful positive effect on someone's day. Amabile and Kramer encourage us to see the value in spotting and celebrating the small wins as a major contributor to the feeling that we're making progress at work.

WIN OF THE WEEK

If something has gone wrong and it's a team effort to turn things around, it's useful to consider how you could create shared optimism across the group. 'Win of the week' is a simple way to create collective confidence and build shared self-belief. This action has been so popular with many of the teams we work with, including our own organization, that they now do this every week. In each week there will be highs and lows to navigate, mistakes will get made, things will go wrong, and unexpected challenges will come our way. Win of the week is a way to guarantee that you end your week with optimism. The chance to read and celebrate other people's wins as well as our own leaves everyone feeling positive about progress and motivated to keep going.

What Will I Learn?

Learning in hard moments leads to better judgement.

When things go wrong it can cloud our judgement. It's hard to see a situation clearly in a difficult moment. We might get distracted by insignificant details or spend too much time ruminating about what we wish we'd done differently. Without good judgement, we're less able to make a well thought through recommendation, or take an action that's going to make things better.

When things go wrong, how you respond is often more memorable to the people you work with than the mistake you've made. By taking accountability, zooming out, reflecting and staying optimistic, you will learn in a way that improves your judgement. Not only do you become more resilient, but you build your reputation as someone who can do hard things. Challenges are a part of any role; it doesn't matter how good you are, dealing with mistakes and failure will be a repeated feature of your career. When you learn like a lobster, you see each challenge as a chance to grow, and you become more resilient as a result.

LEARNING WHEN THINGS GO WRONG: SUMMARY

1. When things go wrong, it's easy to respond in a way that closes down the possibility of learning. This might look like avoiding or overanalysing the issue, or blaming ourselves or other people. Reframing our response is how we start learning when things go wrong.

2. Replacing blame with accountability is how we can learn from, rather than repeat, the mistakes that we all make. An action like sharing small-mistake moments across a team can support us to move on from what went wrong while taking the learning with us.

3. Zooming out gives us perspective and is particularly useful when there's complexity and emotion surrounding what's gone wrong. You can practise getting distance from a situation quickly, using a range of techniques, including: third-person viewpoint, fly-on-the-wall facts, swap shoes and time travel questions.

4. Using WWW/EBI (what worked well / even better if) is a fast and flexible way of reflecting in real time when things go wrong. This technique works well whether you're in a surprise, team or long-haul hard moment.

5. When things go wrong, our thoughts can get in the way of learning. Working with our worries by identifying what's within and outside our control will support you to stay calm at a tough time.

6. Recognizing and recording your very small successes, or a win of the week, is a practical way to boost your optimism when things go wrong.

How to Learn When Things Go Wrong

7. When things go wrong, how you respond is more memorable than the mistake you've made. Taking accountability, zooming out, reflection and optimism will improve your judgement and build your reputation as someone who can do hard things.

DIVE INTO LEARNING LIKE A LOBSTER
- Begin by: writing down three very small successes at the end of each day for a week.
- Then try: sharing your mistake moments with a trusted colleague or team for a month.

Part 3

Lead Your Own Learning

'Learning is not done to you; it is something you choose to do.'

Seth Godin

If you're not already impressed by the lobster, this final feature might convince you. There's a reason you won't find many lobster shells washed up on the beach: they've probably been eaten . . . by the lobster itself. When the lobster moults and loses its old shell, it needs to replenish its resources quickly. Rather than relying on more unpredictable food sources, the lobster eats its old shell, which is packed full of calcium. It turns out that the lobster is a master of recycling and resourcefulness. Its past self provides fuel for its present growth.

> **A lobster doesn't wait or hope that it will grow, it takes matters into its own claws.**

When we learn like a lobster, we lead our own learning. We recognize that no one should care about or be more committed to our learning than we are. Like the lobster, we don't wait for growth to come to us; instead we become self-fuelling and take advantage of every opportunity to learn. When you lead your own learning, you are making the choice to grow in small and significant ways. To grow by yourself and to support other people's growth. To grow even when it feels difficult. When you learn like a lobster you never leave learning to chance.

Why Leading Your Own Learning Will Help You Grow

> **'Don't wait for the right opportunity; create it.'**
> **GEORGE BERNARD SHAW**

Leading your own learning puts you in control of creating opportunities to grow. You don't need to wait for someone to tell you what to learn or when you can do it. Instead, you look for the learning that's all around you, all the time. Where other people may feel their learning is constrained by where they work or who they work for, people who lead their own learning use their creativity to find a way forward and never stop growing.

Leading your own learning makes it personal to you and energizing to do. You recognize that learning doesn't have to be formal or look the same for everyone. Learning in your own way feels fulfilling and opens up opportunities for your future.

What Stops Us Leading Our Own Learning?

> 'The most pressing task is to teach people how to learn.' PETER DRUCKER

There are three common blockers that act as a barrier to leading our own learning:

1. **Overwhelm:** too many options on what to learn can leave us feeling lost.
2. **Expertise:** relying on what we already know can make us closed to new learning.
3. **Waiting:** when our development is dependent on other people or departments.

There's no shortage of knowledge available, and the options on what to learn are endless. However, too much choice can get in the way of our ability to get started. The volume of topics and skills feels overwhelming, and we get lost in the search for a 'right' decision. It feels so hard to know what to learn that we end up getting stuck.

The second blocker to leading our own learning is when our expertise goes into overdrive, described by scientists as the 'earned dogmatism' effect. When we see ourselves as an expert, we become more rigid in our thinking and less likely to consider new points of view. Perceiving ourselves as an expert means that we opt out of learning, believing that we already have the knowledge that we need. This can sound like:

Learn Like a Lobster

- *This will be useful for my team but not for me.*
- *I've learned this already.*
- *I'm an expert, so this doesn't apply to me.*

The final barrier, and perhaps the one that's most embedded from our ladder-like experience, is waiting for learning to come to us, instead of seeking it out. At school we waited for teachers to tell us what to learn, and now perhaps we wait for our managers or an HR department to do the same. If we make our development dependent on other people, we get stuck. Leading your learning means you create your own curriculum and are your own teacher. Everyone needs support with their learning, but the catalyst for your learning is you.

> *'Regardless of your past achievements and your present level of expertise, your future depends on your ability to keep learning.'*
> Tomas Chamorro-Premuzic

How to Lead Your Own Learning: Make a Start

The only way to lead your own learning is to start. Start small, with an action you feel confident you can make happen. This could look like spending five minutes experimenting with a new technology, watching a TED talk, or getting in touch with someone to have a curious career conversation. Taking one action today is always better than waiting for tomorrow.

In Part 3 we suggest how different approaches to learning can be used in your work today. Perhaps you've been in your role for a while and want to find opportunities to be a *Beginner*. Maybe you have tried leading your own learning but hit a roadblock, so *Adapting* feels useful. Or you might want to rediscover the joy of learning, so *Playing* feels like the right place to start.

We share lots of different ways that you can lead your own learning. Whether that's finding some small firsts in the role that you're in today, introducing some play to your team time together, or redesigning how you rest so you have the energy to learn. Your learning is personal to you; there is no set formula to follow. You have the freedom to design your development in a way that feels relevant to your role today and reflects your aspirations for the future.

We haven't included experimenting and questioning in this section, as we cover these skills in Chapters 1 and 2. They are also both brilliant ways to lead your own learning so if that feels useful for you, it's worth going back to those sections of the book.

CHAPTER 6

Seven Ways to Lead Your Own Learning

There are limitless ways you can lead your own learning, but we've picked out seven options to make it easy for you to get started with at least one. Different learning can be useful depending on the situation, for example if you've got comfortable in a role you could stretch yourself with some beginner-based learning, or if you feel stuck in your silo, connecting with new people might be a good place to start.

SEVEN WAYS TO LEAD YOUR OWN LEARNING

Learning by...	Useful when...	Action 1	Action 2
1. Beginning	*I've got comfortable in my role and want to challenge myself to learn in new ways*	Small firsts	Beginner BHAG
2. Playing	*I'd like to learn in a way that feels low pressure and easy*	Individual pockets of play	Team pockets of play
3. Connecting	*My learning feels too limited to what and who I already know*	Memorable moments	Say yes to a normal no

Learn Like a Lobster

SEVEN WAYS TO LEAD YOUR OWN LEARNING

Learning by...	Useful when...	Action 1	Action 2
4. Giving	I'd like to learn how to help other people	Five-minute favours	Giving equation
5. Adapting	I have constraints getting in the way of my learning	Moving mindset	AI scenario planning
6. Resting	I'm too tired to learn	Active rest	Rest recipe
7. Sharing	I want to make sure I get the most from what I learn	'Learn along' community	Helpful how-to

What Will I Learn?

Leading your own learning is a catalyst for creative thinking.

You can't lead your own learning without thinking creatively. By figuring out how to play, share, connect, adapt, rest, give and begin you will come up with new solutions to your learning, rather than relying on what you've done before. You'll think creatively about how you can support other people to learn, and what to do when constraints mean you need to find an alternative solution. Leading your own learning is how you create opportunities for your career. Like the lobster, you have everything you need to get started with your learning, and once you do, you'll never look back and never stop growing.

'You don't get your CV with your birth certificate; your life is yours to create.'
Sir Ken Robinson

Seven Ways to Lead Your Own Learning

1. Beginning

Learning something new means starting from scratch and wrestling with the uncomfortable feeling of being a beginner. In her book *The Long Win*, Olympian Cath Bishop asks a provoking question: *When was the last time you learned something new?* Attempting to answer this question can prompt a realization that we've fallen into a pattern of more of the same rather than mixing things up. Creating opportunities to be a beginner at work helps us overcome what's described as the 'Einstellung effect'. This is when we default to a familiar solution, even when presented with a more attractive alternative (*Einstellung* is the German word for 'set'). Though familiarity feels comfortable and reassuring, it also limits our learning. Relying on what we've done before makes us less flexible, less creative and results in being closed rather than open minded.[28] And unlike the lobster, who never settles in its shell, we become set in our ways.

The number of beginner moments in our careers is increasing as our jobs continue to change. Though it's intimidating to do something that we've not done before, practising being a beginner means you will build your courage muscle and grow beyond where you are today.

> **Choosing courage over comfort is a critical part of leading your own learning.**

EXPERT INSIGHT: SET A DISCOMFORT GOAL

Researchers Kaitlin Woolley and Ayelet Fishbach have found making discomfort an explicit goal for your growth can be helpful. Being specific about how we expect to feel when doing something for the first time – nervous, anxious, even experiencing dread – means when those feelings happen, we don't see them as a signal to stop but as a sign that we're making progress towards our goal.

> General goal: *My goal is to lead a team meeting for the first time.*
>
> Discomfort goal: *My goal is to try out three actions for the first time that I know will make me feel uncomfortable and nervous, starting with leading a team meeting for the first time.*

How to Begin: Find Small Firsts and Beginner BHAGs

Doing anything for the first time usually comes with at least some discomfort, but making even small amounts of progress on something we haven't done before gives us a sense of pride. Leading our own learning means we don't wait for beginner moments to happen to us but are intentional about creating chances, both small and significant, to try something new for ourselves.

FIND SMALL FIRSTS

When we set out to be a beginner, we often assume it means starting from scratch. Regardless of the skill or talent we're looking to develop, starting with a blank page can feel daunting and intimidating. An easier place to start is to create firsts in the work that you already do. This means spotting smaller and more frequent opportunities to do something for the first time. A fun way to start finding small firsts is to use Beginner Bingo.

- Use the Beginner Bingo card for inspiration on small firsts – you can add your own ideas in too.
- Decide how frequently you want to find small firsts; are you aiming for one a week or one a month?
- Decide whether you want a bingo buddy (someone from your team or a peer in another function) or whether you're going solo.
- Cross off each small first after you've tried something.

BEGINNER BINGO

Lead a team meeting	Use WWW / EBI (what worked well / even better if) for feedback	Have a curious career conversation with someone outside my organization	Add your own ideas
Deputize for a colleague	Spend a day with a different team	Try out some new technology (Miro board, Midjourney)	Add your own ideas
Organize a team day	Deliver a lunch & learn	Use the Pomodoro technique to increase my focus (pomofocus.io)	Add your own ideas

BEGINNER BINGO

Mentor someone	Ask for a LinkedIn recommendation	Use a 5-minute mind map to reflect at the end of every day for a week	Add your own ideas

EXPERT INSIGHT: 'DON'T KNOW' NOTEBOOK

Whenever he began learning about a new topic Richard Feynman, Nobel prize-winning physicist, would start a new notebook and on the first page write *Notebook of things I don't know about*.

Feynman recognized that his notebook provided a place to start learning, even if that learning looked like listing everything he didn't know. When you're at the beginning of learning something new, if you start with a 'don't know' notebook, just the process of making notes will mean you've made some concrete progress. This progress provides useful motivation as we navigate the hard process of learning something new. Continuing to fill in your notebook with your observations, questions and more of what you don't know will give a home for your learning. This makes spotting connections, and also seeing how far you've come, easier and more rewarding.

BEGINNER BHAG

BHAG, a 'big, hairy, audacious goal', was a popular concept in the 1990s. Though BHAGs might not be as fashionable today, they continue to be useful for motivation, energy and to create a clear focus for action. A BHAG stimulates progress and momentum towards something that is exciting and adventurous. Setting yourself a Beginner BHAG will support you to be brave about doing something 'big' for the first time.

We've shared a few examples of Beginner BHAGs below to give you some inspiration for setting your own. The most important feature of a Beginner BHAG is that it has to be something that you haven't done before (or have very limited knowledge of / skill at). If you know the goal but have no idea how you're going to reach it, you can feel confident you're in beginner mode.

EXAMPLES OF BEGINNER BHAGS
- Learn a new piece of technology that until now you've been resisting.
- Start speaking or writing in public: for example, posting on LinkedIn or presenting as part of a community (check out goodshoutcommunity.com for inspiration and support).
- Learn a new skill that you're intrigued by but have never had the confidence to get started with: for example, surfing, chess, a language or an instrument.

Here are some inspiring Beginner BHAGs from people who lead their own learning.

- Journalist Viv Groskop set herself a BHAG of becoming a stand-up comedian by doing 100 gigs in 100 nights.
- Technology entrepreneur Martha Lane Fox, who was left disabled by a car crash, set herself a BHAG of climbing the three highest mountain peaks in the UK and raising £300,000 for charity.

- Author Tim Ferris set a BHAG to go from a beginner to competing in Argentine tango, one of the hardest dances to master, in just six months. With some smart strategies and intensive training, he achieved his goal and won a medal at the Buenos Aires Tango Championship.

> 'It also turns out that BHAGs are something that have stood the test of time. In fact, I can't seem to get them out of my mind – so there is one outstanding question at the end of all this that I keep thinking about – what crazy, scary thing am I going to do next?'
> MARTHA LANE FOX CBE[29]

EXPERT INSIGHT: U-SHAPED LEARNING

> 'It's a good thing to keep bathing in novelty.'
> TOM VANDERBILT

In his book *Beginners* journalist Tom Vanderbilt tasks himself with acquiring new talents. One of his observations, backed up by the research, is that as a beginner your learning is very unlikely to be linear. You are most likely to experience a U-shape where, after some initial learning, you get worse before you get better. Knowing that our path to progress as a beginner is likely to be bumpy can help to keep us going in the moments where we feel disheartened or demotivated by where we are.

BEGINNING: SUMMARY

1. A beginner mindset stops us from getting set in our ways. The frequency of firsts will continue to increase as we navigate our squiggly careers. By being a beginner you will get used to the discomfort that comes with doing something new.

2. Finding small firsts at work will build your beginner confidence. This can be as simple as leading a meeting or mentoring someone for the first time.

3. A beginner BHAG (big, hairy, audacious goal) is something that's daunting, difficult and that you don't know how to do. Setting yourself a Beginner BHAG will support you to do something brave for the first time.

DIVE INTO LEARNING LIKE A LOBSTER
- Begin by: crossing a small first off your Beginner Bingo card this week.
- Then try: setting yourself a beginner BHAG and sharing it with one other person.

2. Playing

> 'Play isn't the enemy of learning, it's learning's partner. Play is like fertilizer for brain growth. It's crazy not to use it.'
> **STUART BROWN MD**

Our working environment and expectations of what work 'is' can feel like a barrier to the idea of play at work. We believe that if we want our work to be taken seriously, we need to be serious. Though we might doubt the value or relevance of play, it's been repeatedly shown that when we have fun at work it reduces stress and increases job satisfaction. As doctor and author of *Play* Stuart Brown says, 'When we stop playing, we stop developing.'

'We are much more likely to love our work when we see it as play.'
Lynda Gratton

Play is a helpful antidote to stress, and though we don't expect work to be fun all the time, small moments of play can reduce the pressures that mount up during a busy day. If you're feeling stressed at work, you're not alone: a survey of nearly 2,000 professionals found that two-thirds of people feel more stressed at work than they did five years ago.[30] Stress can cause us to lose sleep, impact our personal relationships and negatively affect our performance at work. When we play, however, we activate the reward parts of the brain associated with pleasure, creativity and problem solving. By creating play, we manage our stress and in turn create space to grow.

Design company IDEO has recognized that supporting their people to play increases innovation and creativity, which are key skills for their business success. To support play they created 'play dates' – the chance for people to choose something to try out between projects. This could be anything, from creating a newsletter to a new way of using AI. IDEO sees play as a way to give people the freedom to explore, experiment and go beyond obvious answers. One watch-out shared by partner and managing director Michelle Lee is the dread of 'forced fun'. She points out that when playing as a team mandatory participation has a negative effect, and it's important to give people options about how or even if they want to join in.[31]

We might expect a creative organization like IDEO to be pioneering play, but less so a busy emergency department in a hospital. Heidi Edmundson, a doctor in an Accident and Emergency department in London, introduced daily ten-minute learning sessions every week. Each session was a different play activity: for example, a clapping game, a challenge to share a little-known fact, or origami. The positive impact of play showed up in people's wellbeing: more than 80 per cent of people who attended scored themselves as 8 out of 10 on the Warwick-Edinburgh mental wellbeing scale. Sickness amongst nursing staff also dropped by 30 per cent, and staff turnover halved over the year. Edmundson reflects how, beyond the impressive measures, 'Giving staff just a small amount of time and space to be together and have fun was uplifting.'[32]

**EXPERT INSIGHT:
PLAYING IS A SERIOUS BUSINESS**

LEGO's brick-like toys are no longer just for kids. In 2023 a major UK retailer reported that sales of its complex kits aimed at adults had increased by 33 per cent.[33] The LEGO Play Well report found that 87 per cent of adults said play helped them to feel calm, and 86 per cent shared that play helps them unwind from work. In Abbie Headon's book *Build Yourself Happy* she points out one of the pleasures of playing with LEGO is that 'nobody is going to take pictures or give you a score'. You can take the pressure off yourself and simply enjoy the process.

How to Play: Individual and Team Pockets of Play

Creating more play at work is something you can do individually and as a team. Just like when we were kids, we all enjoy moments of play with other people and the freedom that comes from playing by ourselves. Adding playfulness into our work doesn't need to be a radical act. It's more likely to look like creating small pockets of play that can be easily added into your working week.

INDIVIDUAL POCKETS OF PLAY

Designing play into our days will look different for all of us. For example, for some people one hour a week will feel more realistic than fifteen minutes every day. Or you might like to repeat the same type of play each day, or try out something new.

EXAMPLES

- **Games:** pick a game to play every day just for fun. This could be something like Wordle or you can get lots of inspiration from ProtoBot.org.
- **Tech tests:** choose a technology you're interested in testing and have a play with it over a week. For example, you could try Midjourney to create images or Procreate to draw with.
- **Prototyping:** try prototyping an idea you've got or something you're intrigued by. You could sketch your prototype or build it using physical objects you can find in your house. You don't need to share where you get to with anyone – the priority is just to give something a go.

TEAM POCKETS OF PLAY

Team play creates connections and different kinds of conversations. When creating these pockets of play it works best for everyone to be on a level playing field, so no one has expertise in an area. The focus is on playing, not on winning, and play should feel low pressure and easy for everyone to get involved in.

EXAMPLES

- **Desert island crisps:** if you could only take one bag of crisps to a desert island, which would you choose? Even better if you can combine tasting the crisps with talking about them!
- **Spotify playlist:** someone volunteers to be the team DJ. Everyone sends their chosen track to the DJ who puts together a playlist. The DJ samples each track and you guess who it belongs to. Each person then shares why they chose that track.

- **Self-portrait:** everyone draws a self-portrait with their non-dominant hand. Create a team gallery and see if you can guess which portrait belongs to which person. Each person then reveals their portrait by signing their masterpiece.
- **Secret skills:** each person shares one little-known skill. Maybe you used to be a dance instructor, are an incredible knitter, or write science fiction in your spare time.
- **Paperclips:** divide into teams of two or three, and in five minutes see what you can create from a pile of paperclips.

> 'Laughter is a form of internal jogging.'
> NORMAN COUSINS

EXPERT INSIGHT: GRAVITY AND LEVITY ARE NOT AT ODDS

> 'We can do serious things without taking ourselves so seriously, in fact we can often do them better.'
> JENNIFER AAKER AND NAOMI BAGDONAS

When we're laughing, we're learning; and the more we play, the more we laugh. As Jennifer Aaker and Naomi Bagdonas share in their book *Humour, Seriously* humour has a whole host of benefits. It builds bonds, defuses tensions, boosts innovation and bolsters resilience. When we laugh, we release a cocktail of emotions; our endorphins and dopamine increase, whereas our cortisol decreases, making us feel calm. Aaker and Bagdonas remind us that gravity and levity are not at odds. Giving ourselves permission to play at work is good for us and good for our growth.

🔊 Learn more by listening to Jennifer Aaker and Naomi Bagdonas on episode 158 of the *Squiggly Careers* podcast.

PLAYING: SUMMARY

1. Play is a helpful antidote to stress and an important part of learning. Adding play into your day provides a moment of decompression that increases your capacity to learn.

2. Leading your learning by creating play isn't a radical rethink of how you work. It looks like finding small pockets of play for yourself and with other people.

3. One watch-out when creating play with other people is to avoid forced fun. Make sure people have options about how, or even if, they'd like to join in.

DIVE INTO LEARNING LIKE A LOBSTER
- Begin by: playing for five minutes during work today with LEGO or use ProtoBot.org.
- Then try: a team pocket of play such as a Spotify playlist at your next away day.

3. Connecting

> 'In order for us to truly create and contribute to the world, we have to be able to connect countless dots, to cross-pollinate ideas from a wealth of disciplines, to combine and recombine those pieces and build new castles.' MARIA POPOVA

It's almost impossible to get our work done without other people. Every job involves collaboration, but this doesn't always lead to learning. During a working week we spend time with lots of the same people, talking about tasks, projects and processes. And if we do create the space to connect with people outside of our day job, we take the easiest option, which often means sticking with people we already know, and like. Creating connections might feel like a skill you need to relearn as, over the past few years, most of us will have changed how and where we work in some way. This doesn't mean collaboration is harder, just that we need to be intentional about how to learn from people, and sometimes in new ways.

Leading your own learning means recognizing the value in building a range of connections.

Different kinds of connections lead to different kinds of learning.

When learning is the filter for who we spend time with, we become more intentional about the connections we create. We look for opportunities to meet people with different experiences, and think creatively about how to learn in new ways from the people we already know. People are a brilliant source of learning, opportunity and possibility that we don't want to pass us by.

**EXPERT INSIGHT:
WE'RE STILL LONELY AT WORK**

Loneliness continues to be a challenge at work, with one in five employees worldwide sharing that they feel lonely in their jobs.[34] Feeling disconnected impacts our physical and mental health, leading to an increase in time off work and making people more likely to leave their roles. The ripple effect of loneliness goes beyond individuals; in 2023 the estimated cost of loneliness to the British economy was £2.5 billion per year.[35]

Constance Noonan Hadley and Sarah L. Wright's research with over 1,000 workers in the US suggests we need to stop blaming remote working, particular jobs or certain individual characteristics as the causes of loneliness. They discovered that creating a culture of connection by designing simple moments of social connection into the rhythm and ritual of work can have a significant impact on how lonely people feel. Team lunches together once a month, online games added into meetings, social channels on Teams or Slack, were all shared as positive examples of activities that everyone could get involved in and that build relationships over time.[36]

How to Connect: Deep and New Connections

Deepening connections with people we already know helps us benefit from a trusted perspective and someone who believes in our potential. These people can help us learn where we're at our best and how we can be even better.

New connections offer us something different: the chance to discover what we don't know. These relationships give us a window into other people's world, which expands our horizons and helps us to escape siloed thinking. It's harder to pre-empt exactly what we're going to learn from people we haven't met before, but when we're intrigued about the unknown it leads to new ideas and opportunities.

'We need to build relationships beyond the ones that we need right now.'
Margaret Heffernan

- **Deep connections:** explore our potential and offer a trusted perspective.
- **New connections:** expand our horizons and encourage creative thinking.

CREATING DEEP CONNECTIONS: MEMORABLE MOMENTS

Deepening the connections we already have increases the chances that people can spot opportunities on our behalf. These opportunities might be projects, jobs or other people for us to connect with. In our experience, you won't have many deep connections, so the ones that you do have are worth looking after. One easy way to maintain a deep connection is looking out for 'I saw this and thought of you' moments. For example, Helen recently read a trends report on podcasting and sent the link to a small group of podcasters we know well. These are small actions that don't take much time but which show people that you're thinking of them, keeping you at the front of their minds.

Another way to deepen connections is to look for opportunities to create memorable moments. This can be as simple as attending an event with someone or learning a new skill alongside a colleague. A memorable moment creates the space for different kinds of conversations, either one to one or as a group. These experience-based conversations will often be more unstructured, open and wide-ranging than your standard work conversations. Not only are these moments memorable, but they can also offer an opportunity to talk about harder topics with a trusted connection.

EXAMPLES OF MEMORABLE MOMENTS

- Culture connection: visit an exhibition, gallery or see a show together. For example, in a recent visit to London, author Dorie Clark invited Helen to see *Operation Mincemeat* at the theatre.
- Walk and talk: switch a catch-up in the office for a walk and talk outside in a local park or green space. For example, every quarter Sarah has an agenda-less walk and talk with everyone from our company, Amazing If.
- Memorable team moments: if you want to deepen connections within your team, design some shared experiences that are out of your ordinary. For example, in the last year our team have had a go at landscape painting, a cooking lesson and improvisation.

EXPERT INSIGHT: WORK YOUR WEAK TIES

> 'When it comes to finding out about new jobs – or, for that matter, new information, or new ideas – "weak ties" are always more important than strong ties.'
> MARK GRANOVETTER

Research led by Lynda Gratton, a professor at London Business School, found that during the pandemic people gravitated towards spending time with their strong ties (people we know well) and as a result individuals' circles of connections got smaller.[37]

Weak ties (people we have some association with but don't know well) were deprioritized, perhaps in part because these had previously been facilitated by the proximity of being in the office. Weak ties are important, as they give us the chance to connect with a wider community. These connections have new knowledge and, as Gratton points out, it's often here that we find serendipity and generate innovation through combining ideas in new ways.

Gratton suggests that, as work is being redesigned into an increasingly hybrid model, a range of connections, strong and weak, will continue to be important. Rather than relying on being in the office for our connections, experiments with virtual and augmented reality could offer interesting new ways to create new connections and maintain our network of weak ties.

CREATING NEW CONNECTIONS: SAY YES TO A NORMAL NO

It's easier to spend time with people who we know well and have lots in common with. Creating new connections can feel difficult, as it's hard to know where to find new people. Nerves and apprehension about meeting someone for the first time can also get in the way, but new people bring novelty into our learning. They know things that we don't, and they know people outside of our world.

Spending time connecting with people outside of our ordinary creates a catalyst for learning in unexpected ways.

This can look like saying yes to something that you might normally say no to, perhaps because it doesn't feel like a priority, or you aren't sure about the purpose. Your yes works best when it reflects the way you prefer to build relationships. For example, if you're more introverted, a smaller group of new people might feel more appealing. Or if you're more extroverted, an event with hundreds of people might be more energizing.

EXAMPLES OF 'SAY YES TO'
- A group learning experience focused on a topic or subject outside of your usual area of interest. For example, Sarah joined a systems thinking programme, motivated by the people she might meet.
- An event on a topic you're intrigued by but that isn't related to your day job. For example, Helen went to a poetry workshop and met people who all shared a love of language.
- Join a community that brings together people who have a common area of interest but are from different worlds. These communities often stay connected through technology like WhatsApp groups where people share ideas and opportunities. For example, we're in an authors' WhatsApp group, where we're all connected by writing but have very different experiences and areas of expertise.

EXPERT INSIGHT: LEARN TO GET LUCKY

'Serendipity is more likely once we encounter random outside influences.' DR CHRISTIAN BUSCH

Some of the most successful businesses and products, everything from Post-it notes to pacemakers, were created from moments of serendipity rather than rigorous planning. Dr Christian Busch, author of *The Serendipity Mindset*, suggests that by seeding serendipity triggers we can all benefit from 'smart luck'. Triggers can include spending time in unexpected places and proactively searching for new information, resources, people and ideas.

One practical idea Busch recommends is considering how to introduce yourself in a way that creates hooks for serendipity triggers. Busch shares the example of entrepreneur Oli Barrett who, when asked what he does, rather than saying, 'I start up businesses,' responds with, 'I love connecting people (passion), I set up a company in the education sector (role), I'm learning about philosophy (interest), and I've recently started playing the piano (a hobby).' By answering this common question in a more interesting way, Barrett creates multiple opportunities for coincidence and connection.

Three Actions to Create All Kinds of Connection

Connecting is a critical part of leading your own learning and matters for anyone who wants to create more opportunities in their career. We've shared three ideas for action below that are helpful for developing both deep and new connections.

Seven Ways to Lead Your Own Learning

1. RECONNECTION

Reconnecting with someone can be easier than establishing a completely new connection (and can lead to new connections too). What can stop us from reconnecting is feeling embarrassed that we haven't been in touch for a while, but it's worth remembering that most people are looking for more opportunities to connect, not fewer. To make a reconnection meaningful it's useful to remind yourself, and your connection, of something you have in common. Perhaps you both care about the same cause or are working in a similar industry.

2. ANYONE ELSE?

A simple way to create more connections is to end a conversation with an *anyone else?* question, as you never know who knows who. Directly asking people who else they'd recommend you connect with often leads to introductions and new opportunities for your learning.

> 'Thanks, that's been a really useful conversation. Is there anyone else you'd recommend I connect with, as I'm excited to keep learning?'

3. CONNECTION COFFEE

People like helping people. When you ask to spend time learning with someone (whether it's a new, an existing or a reconnection), you'll make them feel useful and valued. Setting a goal at the start of every month to have a connection coffee (virtual or in person) with someone different will give you a prompt to get in touch and see if they can spare you thirty minutes for a catch-up.

- Set yourself the goal of one connection coffee each month (to deepen a connection, reconnect, or connect with someone new).
- Choose three questions to ask in the conversation, to give yourself enough structure to get started; there are some ideas in the list below for you to borrow or adapt.

CONNECTION COFFEE EXAMPLE QUESTIONS

1. 'What does a "day in the life" look like for you?'
2. 'What do you enjoy the most about the work you do?'
3. 'What's the most significant challenge you're grappling with at the moment?'
4. 'What are some of the trends impacting your role or team?'
5. 'What are you interested to learn more about?'
6. 'If you could wave a magic wand, what would you change about your week?'
7. 'What's the biggest mistake you've made?' (*We wouldn't suggest this as your first question!*)
8. 'What motivates you the most about the work you do?'
9. 'Who, or what, has helped you get to where you are today?'
10. 'What do you think would surprise someone/me about the work you do?'

After each connection coffee, write down one insight you want to remember. Keep your notes from each conversation in the same place. Looking back at your learning can help you connect the dots across different conversations, and makes your learning more memorable.

> 'Learning is all about connections, and through our connections with unique people we are able to gain a true understanding of the world around us.'
> PETER SENGE

CONNECTING: SUMMARY

1. Different kinds of connections lead to different kinds of learning. Deep connections support us to explore our potential, while new connections lead to novelty and expand our horizons.

2. Shared experiences deepen connections as they lead to conversations about who someone is, rather than only what they do. Saying yes to something you'd normally say no to is a useful way to create new connections.

3. Three ideas for action to create both new and deep connections are: reconnecting with someone based on something you have in common; setting yourself a goal of one connection coffee each month; ending conversations with an *anyone else?* question.

DIVE INTO LEARNING LIKE A LOBSTER
- **Begin by:** scheduling a connection coffee in the next month.
- **Then try:** designing a memorable moment to create team connection.

4. Giving

> 'The smallest act of kindness is worth more than the grandest intention.' OSCAR WILDE

Giving is good for us, so much so that scientists use the phrase 'helper's high' to describe how we feel after doing something for someone else. For example, a study of 70,000 people in the UK over nearly 10 years found that those who volunteered, versus those who didn't, were more satisfied with their life and were in better health, both physically and mentally. Not only did volunteers experience what researchers call a 'warm glow' but it boosted social connection and built new skills.[38] But giving doesn't have to look like volunteering; it might be giving your strengths to someone else in a mentoring conversation, or as simple as giving your time to listen to a team member who needs a sounding board for a challenge they're experiencing.

Giving to other people might not seem like an obvious way to lead your own learning, but the potential for growth is significant. This doesn't mean giving to everyone all of the time, as that can result in people pleasing or overwork rather than learning. However, when we learn how to give in a way that is unique to us and useful to other people, it results in unexpected growth that's hard to realize any other way.

EXPERT INSIGHT: ARE YOU A GIVER, TAKER OR MATCHER?

Research by Wharton professor and psychologist Adam Grant identified three types of people in organizations:

- Takers: people who try to get as much as possible and give as little as they can get away with.
- Matchers: people who aim to maintain an even balance between give and take.
- Givers: people who help others without expectation of anything in return.

Grant's research found that though most people act like matchers in their professional life, it's actually the givers who are the top performers. Interestingly, givers may also be the worst performers, as some givers can fall into the people-pleasing trap. What makes a standout giver is the strategies they use and choices they make. Grant shares: 'If you're a giver at work, you simply strive to be generous in sharing your time, energy, knowledge, skills, ideas and connections with other people who can benefit from them.'

One way that Grant suggests organizations can promote giving is through an exercise called Reciprocity Ring (originally developed by sociologist Wayne Baker and Cheryl Baker at Humax). This is when each person involved makes a request to the group, and people use their knowledge, resources and connections to respond however they can. The Reciprocity Ring has been run in a wide variety of companies, who share that it has not only saved them money but prompted a 'pay it forward' mindset and an appreciation that everyone has something to give.

How to Give: Five-Minute Favours and Giving Equation

What we have to give isn't determined by the level we're at, or how senior we might be; everyone has something to give. Giving doesn't have to be time-consuming; it can be as quick and simple as introducing two colleagues, or sharing an interesting article with a team member. You learn the most, though, when you give in a way that's personal to you and connects who you are with what you care about. This can be one of the most satisfying and rewarding ways to lead your own learning.

THE FIVE-MINUTE FAVOUR

There are lots of small and fast ways we can give to the people we work with. These opportunities often already exist, we just might not be taking advantage of them. Maybe because we're too busy, or question how useful the action is. Entrepreneur Adam Rifkin has a reputation as an incredible networker. He credits this to an action he calls the 'five-minute favour': doing something quickly for someone else with no expectation of anything in return. We all have the chance to start or increase the number of five-minute favours that are part of our week, and when we do we build a giving mindset into how we work.

> EXAMPLES OF FIVE-MINUTE FAVOURS
> **Thoughtful thank you**
> Say thank you to one person who has made a difference to your development.

Make an introduction
Connect two people together who you think would benefit from each other's experience.

Thought of you
When you read, watch or listen to something that relates to the work of someone you know, send it with a 'saw this and thought of you' message.

Write a recommendation
Offer to write a recommendation for someone on LinkedIn.

Extend an invite
Ask someone to join you at an event.

GIVING EQUATION

You can also lead your learning by giving in more significant and personal ways. This is less likely to be a one-off give, but something you commit to for a longer period of time, such as a mentoring programme or volunteering for a charity. This is where you have the opportunity to give something that's more unique to you. Your unique gives come from the personal passions, talents and skills that you have and the people you feel connected to. The 'giving equation' exercise below will support you to generate ideas for what you could give. You might get to a few answers straight away, but even if you don't, exploring your responses to each part of the equation will put you on the lookout for the right gives when they come your way.

Giving Equation

Passion × Skills × People = My Give

Passion: *what do I care about in and out of work?*
These can be passions in any area of your life, anything from scuba diving to statistical analysis. Or your passion might be related to a societal challenge like social mobility or gender equality.

Skills: *what skills, strengths and talents do I have?*
This can be areas of expertise like coding or editing, or related to your natural talents like listening or empathy.

People: *who do I want to give to?*
People in your team, organization, industry, network, local community, friends, family? Who do you feel connected to? You might want to give in a one-to-one way or be more motivated to give in a one-to-many way.

**GIVING EQUATION:
HOW TO WORK OUT WHAT YOU WANT TO GIVE**

	Passion/s	Skills	People	My give
Example 1	Career development	Enthusiasm Connections Strategic skills	Marketeers at the start of their careers	*Volunteering for Marketing Academy Foundation leadership events to raise money for apprentices*

Example 2	Flexibility at work	Events expertise Relationship builder	Creative industry	*Creating the new work network*
Example 3	Supporting kids (my own and others)	Creative skills Accounting skills Enthusiasm Questioning skills	Local school	*Chair of the PTA*
Example 4	Support under-privileged people in my local community	Time Local knowledge and network Empathy	Low-/no-income people	*Establish a food bank*

EXPERT INSIGHT: INFECTIOUS GENEROSITY

> 'Simple, ordinary, unremarkable human kindness now has the potential to ripple outward like never before.'
> CHRIS ANDERSON, HEAD OF TED

In his book *Infectious Generosity* Chris Anderson proposes a shift in the conventional mindset towards giving. Rather than thinking *if I give, I will have less*, he suggests we should begin with *if I give, I will gain more*. Anderson argues that generosity is in our DNA and is driven by two hard-wired human instincts:

1. the visceral desire to help others
2. the automatic urge to respond to generosity in kind

Anderson also highlights the work of social psychologist Elizabeth Dunn, who has found that *how* we give makes a difference. The benefits of giving spike when people feel a sense of connection with those they are helping and can visualize the difference they're making in individuals' lives. In her TED talk Dunn concludes that we should stop seeing giving as a moral obligation and start seeing it as a source of pleasure.[39]

GIVING: SUMMARY

1. Giving is good for us and other people. When we give in a way that's unique to us and useful for other people, we grow in unexpected ways.

2. An easy give to get started with is adding some five-minute favours into your week. This could look like making an introduction, inviting someone to an event, or writing a recommendation.

3. The giving equation (passion × skills × people) will support you to figure out more significant and personal opportunities to give.

DIVE INTO LEARNING LIKE A LOBSTER
- Begin by: saying thank you to one person who has made a difference to your development.
- Then try: listing three people or groups that you'd like to give to.

5. Adapting

> 'Seize change. Use it. Adapt and grow.'
> OCTAVIA E. BUTLER

We don't lead our own learning in a stable and predictable environment, but one where there's lots of change and uncertainty. Your growth will be impacted by decisions that are outside your control, and you will encounter unexpected challenges that make leading your learning harder than it was before.

There are three common challenges that can get in the way of learning:

1. **Time:** your job becomes unexpectedly busy and there's less time for learning.
2. **Money:** budgets have changed and investment in learning has reduced.
3. **People:** a new leader is appointed who doesn't prioritize or role-model learning.

When these situations occur, we can be at risk of something McKinsey leaders Jacqueline Brassey, Michiel Kruyt and Aaron De Smet describe as the 'adaptability paradox'. In the moment when we most need to adapt, we go back to old approaches that don't work in new situations. To continue leading our learning in moments of change and challenge, we have to adapt so that our growth doesn't stall.

EXPERT INSIGHT: DELIBERATE CALM

McKinsey leaders and authors of *Deliberate Calm* Jacqueline Brassey, Michiel Kruyt and Aaron De Smet recommend responding to unexpected challenges with what they describe as 'deliberate calm'. There are three major elements to cultivating this approach.

1. Learning agility: leaders need to be learners even in the most challenging situations. Brassey and De Smet describe learning agility as staying curious, seeking feedback and learning from experiences.
2. Emotional self-regulation: this is the ability to recognize and manage emotions in a way that supports productive thinking and actions.
3. Dual awareness: this means both understanding ourselves and the situation we're facing.

Brassey, Kruyt and De Smet have shown that deliberate calm can help people not only to overcome unhelpful habits in hard moments but to thrive during uncertain times.[40]

How to Adapt: Moving Mindset and AI Scenario Planning

> 'A constraint should be regarded as a stimulus for positive change – we can choose to use it as an impetus to explore something new and arrive at a breakthrough.' ADAM MORGAN AND MARK BARDEN

MOVING MINDSET

In their book *A Beautiful Constraint* Adam Morgan and Mark Barden discovered that people who are able to adapt to constraints have the ability to move their mindset.

When something gets in our way, we all start in victim mode, which could sound like: *Why is this happening to me?* Then we will often move into how to neutralize the challenge by asking ourselves: *How can I find my way around this?* The best adaptors don't stop there, they move into a transformer mindset, where they see a constraint as a chance to adapt and even arrive at an unexpectedly better solution than they'd originally anticipated.

Morgan and Barden point out that these mindsets are not three different people; we all share the ability to move our own mindset from victim to neutralizer to transformer. Moving mindset means we can start generating alternative actions to lead our own learning when something is getting in our way, and this stops us from getting stuck.

MOVING MINDSET

Learning constraint	Victim	Neutralizer	Transformer
New leader who doesn't prioritize learning	I can't learn now that my leader isn't supportive.	I'll learn in my own time after work.	I'm going to set up a series of lunch & learns so I can spend time with like-minded learners across my organization.

Funding for my coaching course has been cut	I can't fund the learning myself, so I'll have to give up.	I'll wait and reapply for funding in six months' time.	I can get in touch with the external coaching company and volunteer to be a coachee for coaches who are looking for people as part of their practice. That way, I can learn from and create new connections with a coaching community.
I've been put on a new project and now my time planned for learning feels unrealistic	Learning just isn't possible for me right now.	I can still progress my learning plans if I adjust my expectations about how much I'll be able to get done each week.	I'm going to design a learning sprint for myself based on the new project I'm working on. That way, I can be intentional about what I'm learning from this new piece of work.

AI SCENARIO PLANNING

When challenges are unexpected, adopting a transformer mindset is a useful response, but we can also be proactive and anticipate how we might need to adapt our learning. AI scenario planning is a helpful tool to futureproof your learning. Creating scenarios means we can consider risks and spot what could go wrong with our learning. You can use these risks to work out how you would adapt and what action you would need to take. Scenario planning increases the level of control we have over our learning and means that rather than reacting on instinct in the moment, we're prepared and ready to respond.

Generative AI has made creating scenarios and figuring out how you might respond to a constraint or challenge much quicker and easier. By using a scenario planning prompt in ChatGPT and adding your own learning context, you can quickly get some insight into the potential risks and suggested actions that you can take now to continue leading your own learning, whatever the scenario or situation.

EXAMPLE OF AI SCENARIO PLANNING PROMPT

> My role is a *marketing manager*.
>
> I would describe the organization I work in as *a large global bank with a well-known brand that has been established for more than 150 years*.
>
> My learning goal for this year is to *develop my creative-thinking skills, as this is useful in my role today and is a skill I'd like to use even more in future roles*.
>
> What scenarios could get in the way of my learning and how could I adapt in response?

AI SCENARIO PLANNING PROMPT

> My role is a _____
>
> I would describe the organization I work in as _____
>
> My learning goal for this year is to _____
>
> What scenarios could get in the way of my learning and how could I adapt in response?

RESPONSE
(CHATGPT SHARED FIVE SCENARIOS – THESE ARE THREE EXAMPLES)

> Here are some scenarios that could get in the way of your learning goal and how you could adapt in response:
>
> 1. Time constraints and workload pressure
> *Challenge:* Busy schedules and urgent marketing campaigns may leave little time for creative-thinking exercises.
> *Adaptation:* Schedule dedicated creative-thinking time (e.g. 30-minute brainstorming sessions weekly) and incorporate creative problem solving into everyday tasks.
>
> 2. Risk-aversion in a regulated industry
> *Challenge:* Banking is a highly regulated industry, which may limit how creative you can be in campaigns.
> *Adaptation:* Focus on structured creativity – finding innovative solutions within compliance boundaries. Experiment with small creative elements (e.g. storytelling in content marketing) before scaling up.
>
> 3. Team or organizational resistance to change
> *Challenge:* If stakeholders prefer traditional marketing approaches, introducing creative ideas might face resistance.
> *Adaptation:* Use data and case studies to demonstrate the value of creativity in marketing. Start with small wins to build trust and gradually introduce bigger creative initiatives.

CREATE DON'T WAIT

Once you have generated some scenarios, you don't need to wait for them to happen before taking useful action. You can adapt in advance by taking actions that will support you to lead your learning, even if a tough scenario does turn into a reality. In the example we shared, it would be useful for this person to add creative problem solving into everyday tasks and to start small experiments to be more creative now. These actions will never be wasted, they will only add up to even more learning.

EXPERT INSIGHT: DO YOU NEED TO BE FLEXIBLE OR ADAPTABLE?

'In the past we learned one time in order to work; now, we must work in order to learn continuously.'
HEATHER MCGOWAN[41]

In their book *The Adaptation Advantage* Heather McGowan and Chris Shipley suggest a useful distinction (shared originally by Professor Jeffrey LePine) between flexibility and adaptability.

- **Flexibility** is the ability to switch from one tool to another in your toolbox.
- **Adaptability** means dropping the toolbox you have and being prepared to find a new one.

The best adaptors recognize that adaptability requires you to learn something new rather than rely on what you've done before.

ADAPTING: SUMMARY

1. Challenges and constraints, including time, money and people, get in the way of leading our own learning and leave us feeling stuck about how to keep growing.

2. Adopting a transformer mindset means we can view constraints with curiosity and as a chance to explore different ways forward for our learning.

3. AI scenario planning is a useful tool to futureproof your learning. It means you can anticipate what might get in the way of your growth and be proactive about actions you can take now, so you can keep learning whatever scenario comes your way.

DIVE INTO LEARNING LIKE A LOBSTER
- Begin by: identifying what is most likely to get in the way of leading your learning: time, money or people?
- Then try: a generative AI tool to create at least three scenarios that could present a risk to your learning and identify one action you can take now to proactively adapt.

6. Resting

> 'Almost everything will work again if you unplug it for a few minutes, including you.' ANNE LAMOTT

Our relationship with rest is interesting. For some people, rest is a response to working flat out. It's part of a cycle of doing work until you feel drained and then using your weekend or a holiday to recover. For others, rest can feel restrictive; it's something that gets in the way of doing other things that feel more important. Or rest can feel out of reach, and sleep feels like the only possible moment to fit rest in – and even then, it can be hard to relax. In some industries, such as sport, rest is viewed as an essential and unmissable part of achieving and maintaining high performance. As Dr Karin VanBaak points out: 'In order to see gains in fitness, in order for the body to keep doing what you want it to do, you have to give it enough rest to repair itself.'[42]

We might not be athletes, but if we want to achieve gains in our growth, we need to create rest as a ritual and routine part of how we work. Resting is how we build boundaries and prevent burnout.

Leading our own learning means recognizing that rest works for, not against, our growth.

Rest doesn't happen by accident; it requires us to take the lead on defining what it looks like for us and deciding how to make it happen. Learning to rest is what keeps us going and growing.

> **EXPERT INSIGHT: SEVEN TYPES OF REST EVERY PERSON NEEDS**
>
> Dr Saundra Dalton-Smith shares seven different types of rest, which can help us to understand the right kind of rest we need in any given moment (sometimes it might be all seven).[43]
>
> 1. Physical: this is when our bodies need rest. It can be passive, like getting a good night's sleep, or active, which could be stretching, lifting weights or playing tennis.
>
> 2. Mental: needed when we have a busy brain that struggles to disconnect from work. Rest could be turning off your phone for an evening, or a hobby that requires your full focus so you're not tempted to worry about work.
>
> 3. Sensory: prompted by an overload of noise, light and screens. Sensory rest might look like a walk in nature,

working in a quiet and calm space, or turning off your notifications.

4. Creative: needed when we've been under pressure to solve problems and have ideas. Creative rest can come from doing work you're comfortable and familiar with, where you don't have to search hard for the answers.

5. Emotional: emotions, our own and other people's, can be exhausting. Emotional rest might be spending time by yourself, or getting some emotional relief by watching, reading or listening to something that makes you laugh.

6. Social: some relationships revive us while others exhaust us. We need social rest when our relationships become draining. Rest could be spending time with someone you've known for a long time or a group of people who always leave you feeling optimistic.

7. Spiritual: this type of rest is useful when we feel disconnected and are missing a sense of belonging and purpose. Spending time with a community, or contributing to something you care deeply about, can help you to reconnect with this form of rest.

How to Rest: Active Rest and Rest Recipe

> 'Work and rest are not opposites, they're partners.' ALEX PANG

Our work is demanding, which makes rest a must-do if we want to take our development seriously. If we're drained during our work, we're less likely to learn, and anything we do learn is more likely to get lost. Rest is fuel for our learning. This means considering both how we rest as part of the work that we do, and resting in a way that means we can disconnect from work too.

ACTIVE REST

Alex Pang, author of *Rest: Why You Get More Done When You Work Less*, argues that rest is essential for sustained performance and resilience. Rather than seeing rest as simply the absence of work, like a holiday or a weekend off, he advocates for what he describes as 'active rest'. Active rest is any activity that isn't work but where we're fully absorbed and present (and, as a consequence, can't get distracted by work). This can be cooking, dancing, drawing, gaming, exercise or gardening – anything that requires your full attention. Active rest replenishes our energy, and this then shows up in our capacity to learn at work.

It's easy for active rest to feel optional rather than essential in our workdays. We have a busy day and tell ourselves we don't have the time, or an unexpected email comes from our manager, and it feels hard to prioritize active rest over an urgent request. There are some useful tactics you can try out to make active rest non-negotiable.

ACTIVE REST TACTICS

Find a friend

Active rest can be easier with someone else, as we feel more responsible for sticking to what we said we would do. It can also encourage us into active rest even when we're not feeling very motivated.

Signalling

Informally sharing with other people across your team as/when you're off to do some active rest means that everyone gets used to that being part of your rhythm. This is as simple as, 'I'm off for a run now, I'll be back online around one-thirty.'

Forget your phone

If you can leave your phone behind during active rest, you have a better chance of switching your focus and attention. This could be as easy as leaving your phone in a different room to where you're cooking.

Nice nudges

You can make active rest more unmissable if everything you need is ready to go and giving you a nice nudge in the right direction. You might put your trainers on ready for a run, set up the board game you're going to play, or have the right page of your cookbook open.

REST RECIPE

The type of rest we need, and what rest looks like, is personal to each of us. By understanding more about your preference for rest, you are better able to write your own rest recipe and feel confident that by following it you will get the recovery you need in order to learn.

Look at the four questions below and choose the answer that stands out for you.

Seven Ways to Lead Your Own Learning

1. You've had a busy and demanding day at work. Would you rather . . .
   A. Meet a group of people for drinks?
   B. Go home and have some time to yourself?
   C. Spend time with one person who knows you well?
   D. Put on music and do some exercise?

2. You've been firefighting at work for weeks. Would you rather . . .
   A. Go to a work event and make new connections?
   B. Take a day off to forget about work for a while?
   C. Have a meeting with your manager to relook at your priorities?
   D. Spend time in new surroundings – go to the theatre, a gallery, a park?

3. You want to fit 15 minutes of rest into your day. Would you rather . . .
   A. Message your friends for a quick chat?
   B. Go for a walk on your own?
   C. Send a thank-you email to someone who helped you?
   D. Watch a video on YouTube to get some ideas for your work?

4. If you had a full day to rest right now, would you rather . . .
   A. See if anyone you know is around to do something fun?
   B. Have time to yourself, reading, relaxing and switching off?

C. Set up a meeting with your mentor to talk about what's going on at work?

D. Go somewhere you've not been before – try out a new restaurant or event?

REST RECIPE: RESULTS

Count how many times you answered each letter, and find your rest recipe below.

Mostly A's – People Power
Your rest is best when you spend time with other people. You are energized by connection and conversation, and need lots of moments of interaction to help you to recharge.

Mostly B's – Me Moments
Being on your own is important for your resilience. Finding small moments in your days where you can sit in silence and be in your own head helps you to contribute most effectively to your team.

Mostly C's – Sustained Support
You need a small community of people you can trust to talk to. These relationships provide the ongoing support you need to sustain your energy and stop you feeling overwhelmed by your work.

Mostly D's – Energy Escapes
You feel better when you are engaged in mentally stimulating activities. Whether its reading, writing, exercising or spending time in new surroundings, taking your brain to new places creates a disconnect from the day job that helps you to reset.

The rest recipe is designed as a prompt for you to consider how to design rest into your work in the right way for you. When you're intentional about your rest, you will increase your impact and ability to learn.

EXPERT INSIGHT: BEYOND BURNOUT

Journalist and author of *The Burnout Epidemic* Jennifer Moss argues that we need to focus on the organizational roots of burnout if we're serious about addressing the problem. In her research Moss identified that one of the strongest predictors of burnout in an organization is an unmanageable workload, leaving people feeling depleted and demotivated. Moss suggests organizations can address this issue with consistent communications about priorities – including, importantly, what can wait or even not get done. She also suggests a more intentional approach to not only the number of meetings but the format of meetings: for example, switching some calls to be audio only, to give people a break from being onscreen.

Moss highlights a simple way-out that leaders and managers can look for. One study found that when asked the question, 'How are you doing?' people say, 'I'm fine,' on average fourteen times a week, though only 19 per cent really mean it.[44] When employees feel safe and supported, they are more likely to go 'off-script' and share how they're really feeling. Managers can prompt this by asking more specific questions like, 'What's feeling frustrating at the moment?' and sharing their own difficulties, to signal that it's okay to not be okay.

🔊 Learn more by listening to Jen Moss talking to Sarah about burnout on episode 288 of the *Squiggly Careers* podcast.

RESTING: SUMMARY

1. Learning to rest is good for our growth. Resting builds the boundaries that give us the chance to recharge and prevent burnout.

2. Adding active rest into your week, which can be anything from gaming to gardening to go-karting, is one way to give your brain a break from work by being fully focused and absorbed in a very different kind of activity.

3. Working out what rest looks like for you, and what kind of rest you need in different moments, means you can make resting a personal and unmissable part of your week.

DIVE INTO LEARNING LIKE A LOBSTER
- Begin by: filling out your rest recipe.
- Then try: adding one more active rest activity into your week.

7. Sharing

There are lots of reasons why we don't share what we know and learn with other people. Sometimes, it's a lack of confidence; we worry that we're not expert enough, or that sharing our insights might make us look like a 'know-it-all'. For some people knowledge feels like power, and giving it away risks reducing influence and competitive advantage. Often, though, what stops us sharing is that we don't know how to do it. There isn't a clear meeting or moment in the week where it feels like the right time to share, so we keep our learning to ourselves.

Sharing learning is an effort worth making for our growth. When we share what we know, it makes our learning memorable and ensures it sticks in our minds. We also spot gaps in our knowledge, or the areas that we thought we understood but struggle to make simple and straightforward when explaining them to someone else.

EXPERT INSIGHT: HIDING VERSUS SHARING WHAT WE KNOW

Research from Professor Marylène Gagné and her team has found that putting pressure on people to share knowledge doesn't lead to good learning outcomes. Just like forcing kids to share their toys rarely ends well, when we're obliged to share knowledge at work it often backfires.[45] The more an employee feels pressure to share what they know, the more likely they are to hide their knowledge, driven by concerns about losing competitive advantage or receiving criticism from their peers.

However, when employees are autonomously motivated – in other words, they share because they want to – and agree with statements including, 'It's important to share what I know with colleagues,' and, 'It's fun to talk about things I know,' sharing knowledge becomes energizing and something to look forward to.

How to Share:
'Learn Along' Communities and Helpful How-To

In squiggly careers everyone's a learner and everyone's a teacher.

There are lots of different ways you can share what you learn with other people. It might be something you do as part of a group of people learning together, or you might choose to share in a way that's open to anyone who's interested.

'Learn Along' Communities

Spending time with a group of like-minded learners is a great way to share and learn alongside others. 'Learn along' communities often already exist, or you can create one for yourself.

Helpful How-To

This is a way of sharing what you learn in a way that other people can follow. This could be through a step-by-step video or writing a learn-letter. By breaking down your learning, you will both increase your clarity and spot any gaps in knowledge you might have.

'Learn Along' Communities

Spending time in a community of like-minded learners is a safe, supportive and low-pressure way to get started with sharing what you know. The best 'learn along' communities are ones where everyone is equal, with no expectation other than to learn from each other. You can choose how much you want to share, and increase your sharing as you build your confidence.

EXAMPLES OF 'LEARN ALONG' COMMUNITIES

Book/Pod Clubs

Within organizations we're seeing a trend of self-organized groups getting together to learn and share (for example, the food service business Pasta Evangelists read our first book *The Squiggly Career* together and shared insights from their conversation each week on LinkedIn). If this doesn't work in your organization, you could join something like the Rebel Book Club.

Passions

This is when a group gets together prompted by a shared passion. For example, Sarah is part of a small informal community of independent founders who share and learn together over dinner every few months. Or you could join something like The Stack World community, who have a mission to empower women in business.

Squiggly Career Skills Sprints

We've run four skills sprints over the past two years, designed for individuals and teams to take part in and learn together. Over 30,000 people have now spent more than a million minutes learning as part of the sprints. The sprints are free to join and a chance to learn and share at the same time.

EXPERT INSIGHT:
HOW SHARING CAN BREAK DOWN LEARNING BARRIERS

A UK bank noticed that post-pandemic their people were missing out on the chance to learn from each other, particularly the more informal 'osmosis' style of learning that previously relied on being in the same office together. The bank decided to trial a new 'skill swap' event with the purpose of creating an intentional space to share. The format was simple:

- open to everyone in a function to opt into (around 150 people)
- 90 minutes in a room
- 15 minutes in pairs for a skill swap (there were no restrictions, or guidance provided on what people could share)

The feedback from people involved exceeded the organizers' expectations: 'Organization status goes out of the window – anyone can learn from anyone.'

A wide variety of topics have been covered in subsequent skill swap events, from tips on how to run a meeting, to use of a new piece of technology and how to get a mentor. What's been surprising is how much the events create a catalyst for future sharing too, with people staying connected and continuing to learn from each other. Skill swap events are now a regular feature of each team get-together, interspersed with 'topic teach-ins' which are held virtually.

The events have been such a success there are now plans to extend the format to other functions, continuing with the low-key and informal approach that putting just enough structure around sharing has created.

Helpful How-To

How-to guides are popular because there's a clear pay-off for the learner, who can move from not knowing to knowing during the course of one quick video or instruction manual. Turning what you have learned into a helpful how-to guide for someone else will benefit both you as the sharer and also your learners.

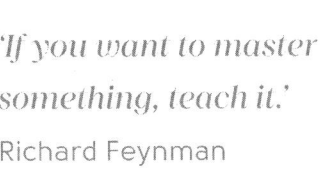

'If you want to master something, teach it.'
Richard Feynman

BENEFITS FOR YOU
- See learning through the eyes of a beginner.
- Organize learning into a structure that will make sense to someone else.
- Practise using simple and straightforward words that are easy to understand.
- Identify gaps in knowledge and understanding.
- Reinforce your learning so it becomes stickier in your mind.

BENEFITS FOR YOUR LEARNERS
- Knowledge is broken down into bitesize pieces that are easy to follow.
- People receive tried and tested learning they can trust.
- People can learn at their own pace, by pausing, revisiting or rewinding.
- There is no delay between learning and doing.

When you lead your own learning, you will start to spot lots of opportunities to create helpful how-to's for your colleagues, team and networks. Technology is an obvious opportunity for helpful how-to's, as other people always appreciate the chance to master a new piece of technology that could make their life easier in some way. A how-to doesn't have to be technology based, though; you could write a one-page summary on how to improve listening skills or run an effective meeting. One example of a helpful how-to that we frequently recommend was created by the host of the *Secret Leaders* podcast, Dan Murray-Serter. Dan took everything he'd learned about podcasting and created a users' guide on Medium, covering everything from getting started to securing sponsorship. Not every how-to needs to be as extensive as Dan's, but if everyone in your team created their own version, imagine how much learning that could unlock.

EXPERT INSIGHT: THINK-PAIR-SHARE

In her book *Uncommon Sense Teaching*, Barbara Oakley explores the think-pair-share approach to teaching. This was originally developed in the 1980s by Frank Lyman, a professor at the University of Maryland. Think-pair-share is a collaborative approach to learning, where students work together in pairs or small groups to answer a question or solve a problem. As the name suggests, there are three stages:

> Think: students get the chance to think through an open-ended question for themselves. They can make notes and organize their thoughts.

Pair: students share and review their ideas in a pair. They might decide one idea is better than the other, or come up with a new improved solution.

Share: students share their conclusions with the wider group.

Oakley describes how the critical *think* part of the process is often overlooked, but this is important as it's when students start to make sense of what they're learning. By pairing up, students have the chance to learn from each other. And by sharing, everyone gets the opportunity to learn from the wider group.

LEARN-LETTERS

Learn-letters are an example of a helpful how-to that will benefit you and other people. When you write down what you're learning, it creates clarity and consolidates knowledge. In the process of writing things down we realize what we do and don't know, both of which are equally important parts of the learning process. You will learn even more if you practise reading your writing out loud, as it can help you spot when something doesn't make sense.

EXAMPLES OF LEARN-LETTERS

- Write a *three things I learned* summary after each learning moment you have (this could be an event, a course, or a conversation) and share it with your team via Slack or Teams.

- Write a newsletter on a subject you're passionate to learn more about, and share it with people so they can subscribe.

Even if only one person reads what you've written, you've still created an opportunity to share what you know. A few of our favourite newsletters for learning are: *Five things on Friday* (James Whatley), *The Imperfectionist* (Oliver Burkeman), *Wonder Tools* (Jeremy Caplan) and *The Week at Work* (Christine Armstrong).

- Write a *read/watch/listen to* playlist every month, sharing with people what you've been learning from.
- Write a post on LinkedIn reflecting on what you've learned from reading *Learn Like a Lobster*, tag us both and share with your followers.

EXPERT INSIGHT: MY AI PROTÉGÉ

The 'protégé effect' describes the boost in learning effectiveness we get from even the expectation of teaching. For example, some computer programmers practise what's called 'rubber duck debugging', where they explain their code, line by line, to a plastic toy.[46] Sharing their code out loud makes it easier to identify bugs they might have missed.

Author David Robson put the protégé effect to the test when learning Spanish by prompting ChatGPT to take on the role of a curious Spanish student, 'Mia', who would like to hear what he was learning. Mia asks questions and follow-ups and, though Robson shares that he initially felt self-conscious talking to a computer, after only a few weeks he was more confident in real-life interactions thanks to his AI protégé.[47]

Robson reflects that, though you might ideally share what you're learning with a real-life person, a rubber duck or an AI tool isn't a bad place to start.

'Articulating our knowledge then helps to cement what we have learned.' DAVID ROBSON

SHARING: SUMMARY

1. Sharing will increase your learning efficiency and effectiveness. It's how you make your learning stick and spot any gaps in your understanding.

2. You can share your learning in a range of ways, from joining a 'learn along' community to writing or recording a helpful how-to. Opportunities to start sharing your learning are usually free, and easy to get started with.

3. Whether you share your learning with ChatGPT, a rubber duck or a thousand people, the more you share, the more learning you'll get in return.

DIVE INTO LEARNING LIKE A LOBSTER
- Begin by: explaining out loud something you've learned in three simple steps to an object.
- Then try: writing a learn-letter about this book to share with your team or on LinkedIn.

Part 4

Lobster-Like Learners

CHAPTER 7

Advice from Lobster-Like Learners

We asked a question of lobster-like learners we admire and have learned from: *What advice would you give someone who wants to learn more at work?*

This chapter shares their generous insights, in their own words. Our learners hadn't read *Learn Like a Lobster* before sharing their wisdom with us, but you will spot lots of the themes that we've explored – questions, curiosity, giving, experimenting, listening and learning from other people – in their responses.

> To learn effectively, detach your identity from your work. Feedback, adaptation and curiosity are easier when your sense of self isn't tied up in outcomes or affirmation. Growth happens when we see our work as evolving, imperfect, and ever improving, not as a reflection of who we are.
> BEN BROOKS, FOUNDER AND CEO OF PILOT INC.

> Don't keep your intention to learn more at work to yourself. Tell the people you work with that you want to grow and develop,

and ask them to be on the lookout for opportunities that will help you do that. People always want to help others, but they won't know to make those connections unless you speak your intention out loud. And don't be afraid to repeat it, because you can't guarantee that everyone will remember it.
AMY GALLO, *HARVARD BUSINESS REVIEW* CONTRIBUTING EDITOR

Hang out with people you typically don't, especially if they have different backgrounds, experiences, values and perspectives. Because one of the most underrated ways to learn at work is to expose yourself to different minds and understand things from other people's point of view.
DR TOMAS CHAMORRO-PREMUZIC, PSYCHOLOGIST, AUTHOR AND ENTREPRENEUR

Seek out the hard! Try hard things, take them on. You will remove the mystery associated with those hard things. And at the same time you will gain an exponential return in terms of your learning confidence. You will discover that many hard things are conquerable and you will discover that when they are not, it doesn't matter all that much. All of that will build your confidence to take on the next hard thing. Learning is a muscle. It takes commitment, willingness to be uncomfortable, willingness to fail. The more you do it, the more conquerable things you don't know (yet) will seem, and the less mystique the world outside your immediate expertise will hold.
CLAUDIA HARRIS OBE, CEO OF MAKERS

Be like a meerkat: always looking upwards and sideways. Talk to people who aren't in your department, people who are in other companies: what's going on? What trends are coming down the pipeline that you need to learn more about? Read widely, and outside your area of expertise. I think curious people are

always going to be open to learning and fresh ideas, wherever they happen upon them.
ISABEL BERWICK, FINANCIAL TIMES JOURNALIST, AUTHOR OF THE FUTURE-PROOF CAREER

Learning more at work means being interested in everything and everyone you work with. Listening more than speaking. Asking more than telling. Embracing all the knotty problems of the workplace with a willingness to try and fail and try again. A successful mindset is one that sees learning everywhere.
OLI DE BOTTON, CEO OF THE CAREERS & ENTERPRISE COMPANY

Just ask! You don't learn by sitting quietly worrying about what you don't know. Ask the questions that come to you, and demonstrate your curiosity and willingness to learn in the process.
RACHEL EYRE, CHIEF CUSTOMER AND MARKETING OFFICER, ASDA

The key thing is to listen, to watch and to volunteer to help – evening events, meetings where an extra pair of hands would be welcome. It's those water cooler moments, when you're learning about work without knowing you're learning, that transform a job into a career. I'm a great believer in working from the bottom up, so you have a true sense of all the nuts and bolts that go to make up a successful project or piece of work. It's also great management training for later in your career – if you've done the work yourself, you'll know better how to manage other people and help them to achieve their potential and the best results.
KATE MOSSE CBE, AUTHOR AND CO-FOUNDER OF THE WOMEN'S PRIZE FOR FICTION

Focus on constantly improving the questions you ask. Think about how useful the current questions are that you use – what did they

help you find out? – and how you could develop even better questions. One of my favourite questions is: when was the last time you learned something new?
CATH BISHOP, OLYMPIAN, AUTHOR OF THE LONG WIN

Be conscious about what success looks like as you pursue it. Let yourself be happy; enjoy being a dreamer and a beginner. And value those who help you and thank them, because nothing planted grows without support.
JP WATSON, THE POUND PROJECT

Be a learn-it-all rather than a know-it-all. Surround yourself with people smarter than you who can share their knowledge and expertise, find coaches who can question your questions and mentors who will answer your questions. But most importantly, remain curious because curiosity will spark the joy in learning.
ÁINE KERR, ENTREPRENEUR AND BROADCASTER

Want to learn more at work? Don't do it alone. Find a 'learning buddy' or a group of people who are also interested, and you can go to events together, share insights and ideas, books and pods. It makes it social and adds perspectives (people will see things differently).
SOPHIE DEVONSHIRE, CEO OF THE MARKETING SOCIETY

To become a learning machine all you need to do is experiment once a day. The experiment can involve doing anything new and different, as long as it gives you some type of energetic kick. One new thing a day keeps dull work away.
CHRIS BARÉZ-BROWN, SPEAKER, AUTHOR AND FOUNDER OF UPPING YOUR ELVIS AND TALK IT OUT

Advice from Lobster-Like Learners

Don't be afraid to ask questions about or challenge things that feel un-challengeable or un-questionable. If you're curious about something, ask how it works and – this is the important bit – ask why it works like that. If there is a good foundation of sense, or process, underpinning how things work, people are usually happy to explain, which gives you a chance to better understand not only the context of your own work, but the context that your colleagues, or even your boss, are working within. That means you have a better foundation if you ever want to explore those roles yourself, and allows you to be more understanding and empathetic to your team as they navigate their work.

SOPHIE WILLIAMS, AUTHOR, TED SPEAKER AND WRITER

Pick one outcome, something you want to get better at. Find someone great and ask them how they do it. Then create a way to deliberately practise it and get feedback.

ROB GEORGE, COMMERCIAL DIRECTOR, FUTURE PLC

When you come across something challenging, new, or if you're not sure how to do it – view it as a great opportunity for curiosity and learning rather than as a stumbling block. There's always so much to learn, no matter your experience or seniority.

CATHAL O'ROURKE, GROUP CEO, LAING O'ROURKE

Don't wait to be given opportunities, find them.

SARAH KILMARTIN, HEAD OF MARKETING, HOTEL CHOCOLAT

You can learn just as much through observation and imitation as by doing things yourself. So spend as much time as you can with people in your organization that you admire and respect.

ROB PIERRE, INVESTOR ADVISER

Don't be a PR manager for your ideas, but a scientist testing hypotheses. You can't learn without that curiosity. You can't learn without that willingness to be wrong.
JAMES ELFER, HEAD OF STRATEGY AND BEHAVIOURAL SCIENCE, MORETHANNOW

If you want to be good at leadership, spend as much time as possible with great leaders. If you want to be good at sales, hang out with the best salespeople. Offer to carry their bags, write their notes, or whatever helps you get close. The more you see what top performers in any trade do, the faster you will discover what you can do to excel.
OCTAVIUS BLACK CBE, CO-FOUNDER AND EXECUTIVE CHAIR, MINDGYM

Don't be afraid to ask others about their learning journey, especially those who you admire. We don't know what we don't know, so by asking people you respect what they are learning, you may spark some inspiration for you.
TOBI ASARE, MANAGING PARTNER, OMD UK, AND AUTHOR OF
THE BLEND

A good starting point is to first identify the person or people you want to learn from. You may not even know, specifically, what they can teach you or help you with – but you admire them and know there's something you want to explore. Find ways to spend time with them and be helpful to them, and you'll pick up an enormous amount through osmosis alone.
DORIE CLARK, COLUMBIA BUSINESS SCHOOL PROFESSOR AND AUTHOR

ASK. Ask questions, ask for help, ask for advice, ask for training. As a founder and CEO, the most important attribute for any of my employees is enthusiasm and passion. Ensuring you are

executing your current job role well, a good leader would be excited about you wanting to learn more and should help facilitate and want to see you fly.
LEMON FULLER, FOUNDER OF LEMONADE DOLLS

Embrace the unknown and don't ever be afraid to show weakness at work. Even the best of us can learn from the people around us – whether that be a new perspective or a skill we know less about – so step out of your comfort zone and engage in different conversations and opportunities. It's where the real magic can happen.
MICHAEL GUNNING, TV HOST AND FORMER PROFESSIONAL SWIMMER

The most successful people aren't necessarily the brightest in the room but they listen and learn better than most. Remember, as Darwin says, it's not the strongest that survive, but the most adaptable. And to adapt, we need to understand what's going on, watch out for change and then navigate a new path.
EDWINA DUNN OBE, FOUNDER OF THE FEMALE LEAD

If you want to learn, move – literally or metaphorically. Move your body, change your perspective, move to a different part of the room, move to a different sense modality, whatever. When you move, you sense different things, and you change your internal body chemistry as well, so this invites new perspectives and insights.
ROBERT POYNTON, CO-FOUNDER OF YELLOW

An absolute devotion to reading is imperative. Books improve your perspective, and that will pay off hugely when you're at work.
SIMONE HENG, AWARD-WINNING AUTHOR AND KEYNOTE SPEAKER

Deliberately push yourself to try projects and roles that you aren't sure you'll enjoy. The worst case is that you learn skills which will serve you well later, but the best case is that you discover you were wrong, and that opens up career avenues you never knew you had.
ZAID AL-QASSAB, GLOBAL CEO, M&C SAATCHI GROUP

Taking yourself out of your comfort zone will make sure you are always learning and stretching yourself. Take on a new project in an area that is new to you; take a new role in an adjacent area; consider an assignment abroad; change company.
MICHELE MCGRATH, EX-CEO, ADVISER, INVESTOR AND MENTOR

Be curious. Be courageous to ask the questions you're afraid you should know the answers to. Be collaborative, never underestimate the good outcomes that can come from being helpful.
HANNAH BERNARD OBE, HEAD OF BUSINESS BANKING, BARCLAYS UK

My advice would be, just get started. There is a paralysis that can come from wanting to try to learn everything you possibly can before you do something, and actually some of the best learning comes from just doing. I'm someone who plans and who thinks and who has strategy. But if I want to try and do something new, I'll do a bit of groundwork, and then I'll just give it a go on a pilot scale, without the pressure of having to be perfect, or without the pressure of having to succeed, but actually with the aim of learning how to do it.
MARYAM PASHA, X EQUALS AND CURATOR OF TEDXLONDON

Learn from others. Take the time to connect with people who have expertise and skills across different areas of the business – finance, marketing, PR and operations. Build a network of

co-workers, mentors and smart people who can share knowledge, challenge your thinking and push you forward.
ADRIENNE ADHAMI, WELLBEING COACH AND AUTHOR

Grow beyond your comfort zone. Pushing beyond what feels comfortable and familiar is where you'll experience the greatest personal growth, development and rewards.
JASON FOO, CEO OF BBD PERFECT STORM

If you approach learning at work like play, it puts you in a very different mindset. Work is serious. Work doesn't tolerate failure. Play, on the other hand, encourages curiosity, experimentation and collaboration; all prerequisites for learning. So ask yourself: what can you do to create a more playful learning environment at work?
TOM TAPPER, CO-FOUNDER OF NICE AND SERIOUS

Be genuinely curious about people who are different from you. Every person is shaped by unique experiences, cultures and influences, so actively listen, ask thoughtful questions, and seek perspectives that differ from your own. Growth comes when we step outside our echo chambers and lean into discomfort to expand our understanding.
LEYYA SATTAR, FOUNDER OF OTHER BOX

What are the limiting beliefs that hold you back? Become conscious of them. And then lean in to them, question them and develop the skills to overcome them. So many of us have limiting beliefs we are not even conscious of. We assume things aren't meant for us, or we don't have the right skills or qualities, or the system won't allow it. What if it is our thinking that is wrong? Dream big, explore the limiting beliefs holding you back, and then break them down one by one.
ROSIE BROWN, CO-CEO OF COOK

My advice would be to dive into everything you can at work, even those jobs you think will be hard or you are not sure you know how to do! Don't be afraid to ask questions and have confidence in yourself, as learning often hides in the places we least expect. Like a lobster tossed into the big blue marine world, I discovered my strengths and passions not by knowing, but by doing, volunteering, and giving it all a go. Remember that everyone started somewhere and had to learn to get where they are in life.

DR CARLY DANIELS, SCIENTIST AND LOBSTER EXPERT

GROW YOUR OWN WAY

There is no finish line to learning like a lobster, no moment where you'll be fully grown. When you learn like a lobster, you grow in your own way, beyond where you are today. You never stop learning, and you never stop growing.

The most important action for you now is to get started. Get started with an everyday experiment, by asking for feedback, or having a curious career conversation. Every action you take will make a difference to your learning, and you can keep coming back to this book if you're ever stalling or in search of some inspiration.

> **When you learn like a lobster the one thing you can guarantee is that you'll grow in return.**

Join the Lobster Library

One of the dilemmas when writing a book about continual learning is how to share new ideas and actions as we discover them. In true lobster fashion we decided to experiment with establishing our very own Lobster Library. In our library you'll find links to all the podcasts, articles and tools that we have mentioned in the book. We'll also share any free opportunities we create to learn and grow, like our squiggly career skills sprints. We're hoping that everyone who joins the library will also share their insights and ideas so we can create a community of like-minded lobster learners.

To join the Lobster Library follow the link using the QR code or head to lobsterlibrary.com.

'I've learned that I still have a lot to learn.'
MAYA ANGELOU

ACKNOWLEDGEMENTS

To our 'book in beta' group – Mike Argile, Martha Arjona, Gemma Atkinson, Katy Barnes, Victoria Belkhyate, Soraia Cerqueira, Frankie Dickson Deane, Mhorag Doig, Hannah Donohoe, Crystal Eisinger, Rosie Fennell, Kathryn Foot, Helen Foster, Emma Hill, Joanne Horton, Julia Joskey, Katherine Karalus, Helen Ketteringham, Helen Marriott, Josie Maydon, Christine Munk, Komal Patel, Sarah Rae, Jo Royce, Matt Vass, Freya Villis, Georgia Wheeler, Ed Willis, Anastasia Womack. You were the best critical friends we could have wished for. Your challenge and feedback were invaluable, and we had such fun spending time together. You kept us going and growing and this book is so much better because of all of you – thank you!

Rachel, thank you for being an early reader. You manage to combine strategic insights with spotting when a comma is in the wrong place. And you did this at the same time as having a brand-new baby to look after. You're an inspiration and a brilliant friend.

Acknowledgements

Thanks to our editor Pippa at Penguin. This is our first time working together and we've really appreciated not only your expertise but that you listened so closely and carefully to our vision for this book. Together we've created a book we're incredibly proud of and we hope you are too.

And thank you to Batya, our US editor: your enthusiasm and energy for us and our book stood out and left us in no doubt you were the perfect partner for us as we share our work with new readers.

Thanks to our agent, Rachel Mills, for being such a brilliant sounding board and for championing *Learn Like a Lobster* across the world.

Our team at Amazing If are nothing short of . . . amazing. They gave us the space and encouragement to write *Learn Like a Lobster*, and at times probably trusted the process even more than we did!

And to all our *Squiggly Career* supporters and sponsors. We're here doing what we do because of all of you.

Finally, there's not a week that goes by where we don't feel lucky to have found one another more than twenty years ago. In a parallel world, our differences could have kept us apart, but instead they have brought us together. We spotted something lobster-like in each other and have never looked back.

ENDNOTES

1. https://learning.linkedin.com/content/dam/me/business/en-us/amp/learning-solutions/images/wlr-2024/LinkedIn-Workplace-Learning-Report-2024.pdf
2. https://www.nhm.ac.uk/discover/are-lobsters-immortal.html
3. https://www.linkedin.com/pulse/want-happy-work-spend-time-learning-josh-bersin
4. https://www.tandfonline.com/doi/abs/10.1080/14640748308402115
5. https://hbr.org/2017/05/talking-to-yourself-out-loud-can-help-you-learn
6. https://hbr.org/2022/12/how-to-fix-collaboration-overload
7. https://hbr.org/2019/01/why-your-meetings-stink-and-what-to-do-about-it
8. https://www.theguardian.com/stage/2016/aug/23/sketch-comedy-works-in-progress-edinburgh-festival-daniel-kitson-bridget-christie
9. https://hbr.org/2018/01/what-self-awareness-really-is-and-how-to-cultivate-it
10. https://hbr.org/2017/09/the-problem-with-saying-dont-bring-me-problems-bring-me-solutions
11. https://hbr.org/2018/05/the-surprising-power-of-questions
12. https://www.theguardian.com/lifeandstyle/2020/oct/24/let-me-finish-how-to-stop-interrupting-and-change-the-world
13. https://www.theguardian.com/lifeandstyle/2020/oct/24/let-me-finish-how-to-stop-interrupting-and-change-the-world
14. https://edition.cnn.com/2023/01/11/health/short-attention-span-wellness/index.html
15. https://umaine.edu/lobsterinstitute/educational-resources/life-cycle-reproduction/
16. https://hbr.org/2011/11/theres-no-such-thing-as-constr
17. https://greatergood.berkeley.edu/article/item/how_biology_prepares_us_for_love_and_connection
18. https://hbr.org/2019/09/why-asking-for-advice-is-more-effective-than-asking-for-feedback
19. https://hbr.org/2021/04/do-compliments-make-you-cringe-heres-why

Endnotes

20. https://www.etsy.com/codeascraft/blameless-postmortems; https://www.merseycare.nhs.uk/restorative-just-learning-culture; https://resolution.nhs.uk/resources/just-and-learning-culture-charter; https://theconversation.com/how-the-brain-stops-us-learning-from-our-mistakes-and-what-to-do-about-it-203436
21. https://www.lboro.ac.uk/media-centre/press-releases/2023/april/how-our-brain-stops-us-learning-mistakes/
22. https://ideas.ted.com/mental-time-travel-is-a-great-decision-making-tool-this-is-how-to-use-it/
23. https://medium.com/hacker-maker-teacher/doing-by-learning-by-david-erixon-c0f1fb4b9446
24. https://www.nytimes.com/2014/01/05/fashion/Three-Persuasion-The-Power-of-Three.html
25. https://hbr.org/2015/04/why-brainstorming-works-better-online
26. https://hbr.org/2022/03/dont-underestimate-the-power-of-self-reflection
27. https://positivepsychology.com/circles-of-influence/
28. https://thedecisionlab.com/biases/einstellung-effect
29. https://medium.com/@marthalanefox/bhags-big-hairy-audacious-goals-5469c9534e78
30. https://www.kornferry.com/insights/this-week-in-leadership/workplace-stress-motivation
31. https://time.com/charter/6291785/the-importance-of-play-at-work/
32. https://www.theguardian.com/society/2019/jan/17/introduced-fun-a-and-e-staff
33. https://www.prima.co.uk/craft/easy-craft-ideas/a42741896/john-lewis-reveals-rise-adult-lego-set-sales/
34. https://hbr.org/2024/11/were-still-lonely-at-work
35. https://www.redcross.org.uk/about-us/news-and-media/media-centre/press-releases/employers-should-exercise-caution-when-encouraging-employees-to-return-to-office-finds-brc
36. https://hbr.org/2024/11/were-still-lonely-at-work
37. https://www.strategy-business.com/article/Maintaining-network-connections
38. https://www.washingtonpost.com/lifestyle/2020/07/29/volunteer-happy-mental-health/
39. https://www.ted.com/talks/elizabeth_dunn_helping_others_makes_us_happier_but_it_matters_how_we_do_it?subtitle=en
40. https://www.mckinsey.com/featured-insights/mckinsey-on-books/deliberate-calm

Endnotes

41. https://www.forbes.com/sites/heathermcgowan/2019/10/29/learning-is-the-new-pension/
42. https://www.uchealth.org/today/rest-and-recovery-for-athletes-physiological-psychological-well-being/
43. https://ideas.ted.com/the-7-types-of-rest-that-every-person-needs/
44. https://www.huffingtonpost.co.uk/entry/im-fine-mental-health-campaign_uk_58358091e4b0207d1916cb7d
45. https://hbr.org/2019/07/why-employees-dont-share-knowledge-with-each-other
46. https://rubberduckdebugging.com/
47. https://www.theguardian.com/books/article/2024/sep/09/the-big-idea-how-the-protege-effect-can-help-you-learn-almost-anything

INDEX

accountability 130, 131–8, 150, 165, 166, 167
  failure and 137–8
  learning and 134–7
  mistake moments 134–7
  'name, blame, shame' cycle 133
  why we don't take 132–3
adaptability 176, 207–14
  AI scenario planning 176, 210–12, 214
  deliberate calm and 208
  flexibility and 213
  learning challenges and 207, 213
  moving mindset 208–10, 213
  paradox 207
  waiting to take action and 212
Adaptation Advantage, The (McGowan/Shipley) 213
Adhami, Adrienne 242–3
advice accelerators 94, 99–105
Anderson, Chris: *Infectious Generosity* 205–6
Angelou, Maya 246
Argyris, Chris: *Teaching Smart People How to Learn* 150
artificial intelligence (AI) 24, 185
  protégé effect 230–31
  scenario planning 176, 210–12, 214
Asare, Tobi 240
Asimov, Isaac 13
attention span 81–2, 85
Atwood, Margaret 139

Bailey, James 156–7
Baréz-Brown, Chris 238
Beautiful Constraint, A (Barden/Morgan) 208, 209
beginning 175, 177–83
  Beginner BHAGs 180–82, 183
  Beginner Bingo 179–80, 183
  discomfort goal 178
  don't know notebook 180
  small firsts 175, 178–80, 183
  u-shaped learning 182
Bernard, Hannah 242
Bersin, Josh 12
Berwick, Isabel 236–7
Bishop, Cath 237–8; *The Long Win* 177
Black, Octavius 240
blame 132, 133, 150, 158, 166
Boser, Ulrich 20
Botton, Oli de 237
brain
  feedback, 'brain-friendly' approach to 99
  neuroplasticity 10
  phone and 79–80
  power of three and 151–2
  writing 153–4
brilliant because (feedback) 94, 108, 109, 124, 126
Brooks, Ben 235
Brown, Brené 91
Brown, Rosie 243
Brown, Stuart: *Play* 184

Index

Buckingham, Marcus 57
Burkeman, Oliver 28, 230
burnout 215, 221–2
Busch, Christian: *The Serendipity Mindset* 196
Butler, Octavia E. 207

Cable, Dan 62
Carter, Carissa 56
Chamorro-Premuzic, Tomas 172, 236
Clark, Dorie 193, 240
connecting 175, 189–200
  'anyone else?' question 197, 199
  connection coffee 197–9, 200
  deep and new connections 191–6
  loneliness and 191
  memorable moments 175, 192–3
  reconnection 197
  say yes to a normal no 175, 194–5
  smart luck 196
  three actions to create 196–9
  walk and talk 193
  weak ties 193–4
conversational narcissism 113–14
Cousins, Norman 188
Covey, Stephen 26
creativity 59, 60, 64, 103
  creative thinking 59, 64, 169, 176, 192
  play and 185
Curran, Thomas 26

Dalton-Smith, Saundra 215–16
Daniels, Carly 244
data for your development 6, 12, 55–85
  development areas 56–7
  examples of 56
  listening data 65–74 *see also* listening
  productivity data 74–83 *see also* productivity
  strengths data 57–64 *see also* strengths
  decision/discussion agendas 16, 21, 22–3, 31

deep work day 57, 82–3
default learning 10
Dekker, Sidney 132
Deliberate Calm (Brassey/De Smet/Kruyt) 208
Deming, W. Edwards 33
Devonshire, Sophie 238
discomfort goal 178
distancers/self-distanced perspective 131, 139–45
  fly-on-the-wall facts 139, 141–2, 166
  swap shoes 139, 142–3, 166
  third-person viewpoint 139, 140, 166
  time travel/episodic future thinking (EFT) 139, 143–5
doing by learning 148
Drucker, Peter 171
Duckworth, Angela 155
Dunn, Edwina 241
Dunn, Elizabeth 206
Dweck, Carole 118

Edinger, Scott 64
Edmondson, Amy: *Right Kind of Wrong* 137–8
Edmundson, Heidi 185
Einstellung effect 177
Elfer, James 240
empathy 45, 59, 93, 204, 205
energy audit 56–9, 85
Epictetus 159
Erixon, David 148
Etsy 'Second Stories' 133
Eurich, Tasha 40
Even Better If? (EBI). *See* What Worked Well? (WWW)/Even Better If? (EBI)
experiments, everyday 6, 12, 13–31
  experiments leading to learning 14, 30
  'I Don't Have Time to Think in My Week' 16–20
  experiment 1: to-think lists 16, 17–18, 31

Index

experiment 2: out-loud and quiet thinking 16, 17, 19–20
'I Have Too Many Meetings and They Don't Feel Useful' 20–23
  collaboration causing overload 21, 22
  double-booked meetings 22
  experiment 1: decision/discussion agendas 16, 21, 22–3, 31
  experiment 2: subtraction 16, 21, 24
  overrating meetings 23
  fractured time 22
'I'm Not Making Progress on My Priorities' 24–9
  experiment 1: minimum useful progress 16, 25–8, 31
  experiment 2: no-cabulary 16, 25, 28–9, 31
  perfectionism 25–6, 31
  'work in progress' shows 28
learn-as-you-go experiments 14–15
self-explaining 20
spotting opportunities to experiment 14, 15–29, 30–31
expertise, learning and 171, 172
Eyre, Rachel 237

failure 130, 134
  courage to reflect on 156–7
  growth and 88
  healthy/intelligent 137–8
feedback 6, 91–126
  asking for 95–105
    advice accelerators 94, 99–105
    framing 94, 95–9, 125
  giving 105–17
    accelerating growth with 108
    brilliant because 94, 108, 109–10, 124, 126
    conversational narcissism 113–14
    emotional insight 114–15
    'feedback sandwich' technique 107–8
    praise, receiving/responding to 110
    red flags 105–8
    say the hard thing 94, 108, 110–17, 125
    how to put learning first and 94, 124
  receiving 118–24
    defeatist/defensive/dismissive response 118
    multiplier effect 120–23
    'name it, to tame it' 120
    think/feel/do 119
  'what if?' feedback fears 92–4
Ferris, Tim 182
Feynman, Richard 180, 227
Fiorina, Carly 55
Fishbach, Ayelet 178
Flett, Gordon 25–6
fly-on-the-wall facts 139, 141–2, 166
Folkman, Joseph 64
Foo, Jason 243
fractured time 22
Fuller, Lemon 240–41
future thinking 145

Gagné, Marylène 223
Gallo, Amy 235–6
George, Rob 239
Gilbert, Dan 3
giving 176, 200–206
  five-minute favours 202–3
  givers, takers and matchers 201
  giving equation 202–5
  helper's high 200
  infectious generosity 205–6
Godin, Seth 169
Goldsmith, Oliver 1
Goleman, Daniel 92
Granovetter, Mark 193
Grant, Adam 47, 201
Gratton, Lynda 184, 194
Gregorek, Jerzy 94
Groskop, Viv 181
Gunning, Michael 241

Index

Hadley, Constance Noonan 191
Harari, Yuval Noah 17
hard moments, learning in 1, 6, 87–168
   accountability and 132–8 *see also* accountability
   better judgement and 165
   feedback and 91–126 *see also* feedback
   growth, learning in hard moments and 89
   how to learn in hard moments 90, 127–68
   learning reframes 129–30
   limiting responses 127–9
   optimism and 157–67 *see also* optimism
   reflecting 146–56 *see also* reflecting
   zooming out 138–44 *see also* distancers/self-distanced perspective
Harris, Claudia 236
Harvard Business Review 43–4, 236
Headlee, Celeste 113–14
Headon, Abbie: *Build Yourself Happy* 186
heavy learners 12
Heffernan, Margaret 192
Heng, Simone 241
heuristics 134
Hewitt, Paul 25–6
Humour (Aaker/Bagdonas) 188

IDEO 185
interruption
   audit 57, 66, 68–70
   giving feedback about 116–17
   no-interruption meetings 57, 66, 72–4

job crafting 56, 62–4
Jobs, Steve 12
Johnson, Samuel 53
Just Culture 133

Keller, Helen 157
Kerr, Áine 238

Kilmartin, Sarah 239
King, Billie Jean 35
Kline, Nancy: *Time to Think* 68, 72
Kross, Ethan 34, 140, 141
Krznaric, Roman 45

labelling learning 11
ladder-like learning, letting go of 3–5, 172
Lamott, Anne 214
Lane Fox, Martha 181, 182
Lauder, Estée 74
leading your own learning 6, 169–231
   creative thinking and 169, 176
   growth and 170
   lobster and 169–70, 176
   seven ways of 6, 175–231
      1. Beginning 175, 177–83 *see also* beginning
      2. Playing 175, 184–9 *see also* playing
      3. Connecting 175, 189–200 *see also* connecting
      4. Giving 176, 200–206 *see also* giving
      5. Adapting 176, 207–14 *see also* adaptability
      6. Resting 176, 214–22 *see also* resting
      7. Sharing 176, 222–31 *see also* sharing
   starting 172–3
   what stops us from 171–2
learning as you go 6, 9–86
   data for your development 6, 12, 55–85 *see also* data for your development
   experiments, everyday 6, 12, 13–31 *see also* experiments, everyday
   growth and 10–11
   heavy learners 12
   how to learn as you go 11
   questions to uncover learning 12, 33–54 *see also* questions to uncover learning
   what gets in the way of 11

Index

Lee, Bruce 9
Lee, Michelle 185
LEGO 186, 189
listening 65–74, 228, 235
   cognitive diversity and 71
   improvisation and 67–8
   interruption and 68–74 *see also* interruption
   listening:talking ratio 56, 57, 66–7, 85
   people pie charts 57, 66, 70–72
Littlefield, Christopher 110
Lobster Library 245–6
lobsters
   advice from lobster-like learners 5, 6, 235–44
   fuel their own growth 1, 5, 9–10
   growth in hard moments 1, 87–90, 127
   leading learning 169–70
   moulting 9–10, 87–8, 169
Logan, Brian 28
Lyman, Frank 228

Mark, Gloria 81–2
Maslow, Abraham 129
McGonigal, Jane 145
McGrath, Michele 242
McKinsey 207, 208
Mersey Care NHS Foundation Trust 133
Microsoft Perspectives 99
minimum useful progress 16, 25, 26–8, 31
mistake moments 131, 134–7, 166, 167
Moss, Jennifer: *The Burnout Epidemic* 221
Mosse, Kate 237
multiplier effect 120–23
Murphy, Kate: *You're Not Listening* 67, 68
Murray-Serter, Dan 228

'name, blame, shame' cycle 133
'name it, to tame it' 120

Nawaz, Sabina 46
Newport, Cal: *Slow Productivity* 82
NHS 133
no-cabulary 16, 25, 28–9, 31
No Hard Feelings (Duffy/Fosslien) 114–15

O'Rourke, Cathal 239
Oakley, Barbara: *Uncommon Sense Teaching* 228–9
Obama, Michelle 89
optimism 130, 131, 157–67
   learning in hard moments and 165
   pessimism and 157–9
   power of bad 158–9
   small successes 161–4
   working with worries 159–61
out-loud and quiet thinking 16, 17, 19–20
overwhelm 17, 80, 105, 112, 113, 136, 141, 171, 220

Pang, Alex: *Rest: Why You Get More Done When You Work Less* 216, 217
Parrish, Shane 19
Pasha, Maryam 242
'pay it forward' mindset 201
Pearson, Mary E. 87
people pie charts 57, 66, 70–72
perfectionism 25–7, 31
pessimism 129, 130, 157–60
phone 77–80, 215, 218
Pierre, Rob 239
playing 175, 184–9
   adults and 186
   gravity and levity 188
   individual and team pockets of 186–8
Popova, Maria 189
Porter, Jennifer 38
Power of Bad, The (Baumeister/Tierney) 158–9
Poynton, Robert 75, 76, 241
Price, Catherine: *How to Break Up with Your Phone* 79

Index

productivity 20, 56, 57, 74–83, 85
   attention span 81–2
   decision making, data for development and 83–4
   deep work day 57, 82–3
   phone, breaking up with 79–80
   smart time 57, 75, 77–80
   speed vs space 57, 75–7
   sticking power 57, 75, 80–82
Progress Principle, The (Amabile/Kramer) 163–4
ProtoBot.org 187, 189

al-Qassab, Zaid 242
questions to uncover learning 12, 33–54
   coach yourself questions 33, 34–40, 54
      pairs 38–9
      three principles of 35–7
      using 38–9
      when to add into your day 40
   conversational questions 34, 47–52
      learning and liking, questions increasing 48–9
      question menus 49–52
      question range 47–8
   curiosity and 53
   situational questions 34, 40–47
      clumsy, sneaky or attack questions 41
      'don't bring me problems, bring me solutions' phrase 46
      empathy and 45
      friction and 44
      goals, matching questions with 43–4
      going round in circles 42–3
      pulled in different directions 45–6
      when/then questions 42–7

Reciprocity Ring 201
reflecting 146–56
   balancing thinking and doing for reflection 147–8
   courage to reflect on failure 156–7
   doer preference and 146, 147
   doing by learning 148
   reflecting in real time 148–9, 151
   teaching smart people how to learn 150
   thinker preference and 147
   What Worked Well? (WWW)/ Even Better If? (EBI) 148–52 *see also* What Worked Well? (WWW)/ Even Better If? (EBI)
Rehman, Scheherazade 156–7
resting 176, 214–22
   active rest 176, 216–18, 222
   burnout 215, 221–2
   growth and 214, 222
   rest recipe 176, 218–21, 222
   types of rest/right kind of rest 215–16, 222
Rifkin, Adam 202
Robinson, Sir Ken 176
Robson, David 230–31
Rogelberg, Steven G. 23
role models 132

Sattar, Leyya 243
say the hard thing 94, 108, 110–17, 125
Secret Leaders podcast 228
self-explaining 20
Senge, Peter 199
sharing 176, 222–31
   how to share learning 224, 227–8
   'learn along' communities 224–5
   learn-letters 229–30, 231
   learning barriers and 226
   protégé effect 230–31
   think-pair-share 228–9
Shaw, George Bernard 170
Shopify 21, 24
short-termism 132–3
Siegel, Dan 120
skill swap event 226
Spielberg, Steven 65
Spotify 187, 189
squiggly career 3, 4–5, 156, 183, 224, 225, 246

Index

Squiggly Careers podcast 23, 26, 41, 45, 68, 71, 114, 115, 120, 138, 141, 148, 188, 221
strengths 57–64
  comparison and 61
  cross-training complementary skills 64
  energy audit 56–9, 85
  job crafting 56, 62–4
  personal best 56–8, 61–2, 84
  super strengths 58
  what three words 56–8, 60
subtraction 16, 21, 24
swap shoes 139, 142–3, 166
Syed, Matthew: *Rebel Ideas* 71

Tapper, Tom 243
third-person viewpoint 139, 140, 166
time travel/future thinking 139, 143–5
to-think lists 16, 17–18, 31

VanBaak, Karin 214–15
Vanderbilt, Tom: *Beginners* 182
very small successes 131, 161–4, 166, 167
victim and villain stories 142

waiting, learning and 171, 172

Wakeman, Cy: *Reality-based Leadership* 142
Watson, JP 238
Wetzler, Jeff: *ASK* 41
what three words 56–8, 60
What Worked Well? (WWW)/Even Better If? (EBI) 148–56
  brain writing and 153–4
  how to use 151–5
  long-haul hard moment 154–5
  multiplied by people and progress 155–6
  multiplied by the power of three 151–3
  reflecting and *see also* reflecting
  surprise hard moment 151–2
  we're in it together hard moment 153–4
Wilde, Oscar 200
Williams, Serena 127
Williams, Sophie 239
win of the week 164, 166
Wittgenstein, Ludwig 14
Woolley, Kaitlin 178
Wright, Sarah L. 191

Zenger, John 64
zooming out 138–44